The Afro-American Slaves:

Community or Chaos?

Edited by

Randall M. Miller, A.B , M.A., Ph.D.
Department of History
Saint Joseph's University, Philadelphia

ROBERT E. KRIEGER PUBLISHING COMPANY
MALABAR, FLORIDA
1981

Original Edition 1981

Printed and Published by
ROBERT E. KRIEGER PUBLISHING COMPANY, INC.
KRIEGER DRIVE
MALABAR, FLORIDA 32950

Copyright © 1981 by
ROBERT E. KRIEGER PUBLISHING COMPANY, INC.

Printed in the Untied States of America

Library of Congress Cataloging in Publication Data

Main entry under title:

The Afro-American Slaves.

    Bibliography: p.
    1. Slavery in the United States—History—Addresses, essays, lectures.   2. Afro-Americans—History—To 1863—Addresses, essays, lectures.   I. Miller, Randall M.
[E441.A34 1981]   973'.0496073   80-24034
ISBN 0-89874-078-9

For my father

Contents

Introduction

The character Henry in Martin R. Delany's novel, *Blake, or the Huts of America,* was right when he observed that *"We must take the slaves, not as we wish them to be, but as we really find them to be."*

Where were the real slaves—in the fields, in the big house, or among their own people in the slave quarters? Plantation slavery in the United States was not monolithic. Slave experiences were not uniform or universal. The institution of slavery evolved over two centuries in the South, and the character and composition of the enslaved changed as the institution changed. The institution varied according to time and place; it varied according to the size of the slaveholding unit and the nature of slave employment; and, most of all, it varied according to the individual masters and slaves whose lives intersected in countless complex ways. The vagaries of personal mood and temperament governed slavery as much as any slave code. Still, individual responses to slavery for both black and white operated in a larger context of social relations and approval. For the slaves, the impact of bondage hinged as much on their insulation from the master as it did on the master's coercive power. The slave's family, his faith, and his community life all defined his personal values and provided the means to adjust to the fact of servitude.

The nature and function of the slave community—and so too,

1

the nature and function of the slaves' responses to bondage—are the subject of this book.

American plantation slavery was a contradictory institution. In law, the slaves were property, almost wholly subject to the master's will. In fact, the slaves were humans, who regularly challenged the master's law and will. The contradiction between law and practice, between master and slave, shaped the South's peculiar institution and those whites and blacks caught in it.

Slavery was a violent institution. Personalities clashed and profit superseded paternalism. Masters whipped, and worse. They sold incorrigible slaves as well as superfluous ones. For their part, the slaves defied masters who pushed them too hard, who abused them with rough treatment, or who invaded their cabins and quarters to disrupt their families and community. Slaves ran away, dissembled, broke tools, stole, committed arson, and murdered. They did these things often enough to convince masters that they were *"a troublesome property."* Slavery rested on the threat of force to make the slaves stand in fear, but it also evoked forceful resistance which made masters fearful of the slaves. This undercurrent of fear influenced the human interactions in slave society.

The master's power was not absolute. The whip and the auction block were ubiquitous in the slave South, but masters could not, and did not, rely on physical coercion and sale alone to control the slaves. Good labor management on plantations dictated adequate attention to the physical needs of the slaves—food, clothing, shelter, health care—and reliance on incentives and rewards to spur the slaves to productivity. The conventional morality of their day and the prevailing standards of decency among slaveholders and slaves also constrained masters. However much they failed in fact, masters generally wanted their slaves to regard them as *"de good massa."* The slaves knew this. They manipulated the master's need to provide treatment conducive to productive labor and the master's need for *"approval"* by demanding gardens, increased rations, Sabbath and Christmas holidays, among other "concessions." Thereby, the slaves bid for their own social space.

Slavery was a labor system. Slave work in many ways determined slave behavior and slave culture. Most slaves in the South engaged in agriculture, but the size and location of the farming unit influenced the organization and character of the slaves' work. According to the 1860 federal census, about one quarter of the nearly four million slaves in the Old South lived on farms with ten or fewer slaves. Such slaves toiled alongside their masters in the fields and did a host of other farm chores. Isolated and alone, they did not escape the master's persistent and pervasive presence. Indeed, they often ate with the master's family and bedded down in the same house with them. Over half the slaves in the antebellum South, however, lived on plantations with twenty or more slaves, or put another way, with four or more slave families. One quarter of the slaves recorded in the 1860 census congregated on plantations of fifty or more slaves. The slaves, and the plantations, spread across the South, but they were largely concentrated in the tidewater regions of the eastern coast and in the Gulf states. There they produced the great staples of the South—tobacco, rice, sugar, and, more than anything else, cotton.

Slaves labored from sunup to sundown, year in and year out, with only Sabbath and Christmas holidays off, but each crop set a particular work pace and pattern. Rice cultivation, for example, was best suited to a system in which slaves worked at prescribed tasks. When a slave completed his daily assignment to the satisfaction of the labor supervisor, he enjoyed the remainder of the day off. The stoop labor of rice growing was exhausting, but an industrious, and lucky, slave might complete his tasks soon enough to claim almost half a day as his own. In sugar and cotton cultivation the gang system of labor prevailed. Masters organized the slaves into work gangs to plow, hoe, and harvest the crops. Such collective work was highly regimented, but also rhythmic. Still, spasms of fevered activity broke the rhythms, particularly during harvests. Crops had to be picked or cut in time to avoid spoilation from rain or frost. Children, superannuates, houseservants, indeed all available hands were drafted into the harvest force so that few plantation slaves missed the drudgery of field work in their lifetimes. Most plantation slaves, therefore, shared a common work experience. Yet, perhaps no more than half of the plantation slaves were full-time field hands. The large plantations functioned as almost self-sufficient enterprises, requiring their own handymen, craftsmen, blacksmiths, millers, gardeners, hostlers, domestics, spinners and weavers, and labor supervisors among the slaves. Black plantation slaves entered all areas of production, even management, and thereby gained a measure of control over their own work.

The regular, regimented nature of staple crop production built up standards of performance for the slaves. Masters knew what the slaves could do, and the slaves knew what they must do. But the variety of work, and paradoxically the regularity of work, allowed slaves some room for social maneuvering. Some jobs took slaves away from the white man's supervision. Field hands brought together in gangs talked, sang, and courted among themselves. The regularity of work set time boundaries for the slaves. From sunup to sundown they adopted their public poses for the master. From sundown to sunup, however, they were left to themselves.

Fundamental questions about slavery and its long-range effects on American life turn on what went on when the slaves were left to themselves. Did black Americans create a distinctive culture in the slave quarters? Was this culture a response to slavery alone, or did it derive from other sources? What were the influences of the master, if any, in determining slave, and therefore Afro-American, culture? What is the relationship between culture and social community? How did life in the quarters affect slave personality and the ability of the slave to resist the debilitating effects of bondage? How lasting were the social, psychological, and cultural effects of enslavement on the blacks, and on the whites too for that matter? In short, as Eugene Genovese asks in his essay, what did the slaves do for themselves, and how did they do it? Did the slaves live in community or in chaos? The evidence presented in this book points toward community.

Interpretations of slavery, of course, flow from the kinds of sources historians use. The historical records of American slavery are uneven. They are also maddeningly ambiguous and elusive. Very few documents concerning slavery in the colonial period survive, if they existed at all. Lacking all but a few fragmentary personal accounts of bondage in its formative stages, historians have relied on court records, statutes, and newspaper advertisements to stitch together descriptions of slavery's early development in North America. With careful reading such "public" documents offer glimpses into the slaves' world. In his essay on early South Carolina, Peter Wood uses such documents to show that large portions of "African" culture survived the Middle Passage. Habits of work and numerous technical and agricultural skills comprised part of the cultural baggage enslaved Africans carried to the New World. As slavery became more settled and widespread, it created a larger corpus of records. Gerald Mullin points out that the regimentation of slave work in the eighteenth century required good record keeping on the part of the masters. Also, as planters gained some "leisure" time and became more conscious of their status as planters, they devoted increasing attention to recording their experiences with slavery and with slaves. However self-serving, planters' diaries and letters, judiciously mixed with planters' account and day books and with public documents, provide valuable descriptions of black/white interaction, the means masters employed to assimilate and control the slaves, the means slaves used to resist the masters, and the nature of plantation work. They trace the contours of slavery as a labor and social system, but as Gerald Mullin's comments on slave acculturation show, such documents only scratch the veneer of slave culture. The motives, feelings, and attitudes of the slaves rarely surface.

For the nineteenth century there is an abundance of primary material on slavery, but the credibility of this abundant record is suspect. Much writing on slavery in the nineteenth century was self-conscious, if not polemical. Slavery's vigorous expansion in the nineteenth century propelled the economic prosperity and physical growth of the nation, but it forced the republic into a painful moral and political dilemma. The debate over slavery, which dominated public life in America from the 1830s through the Civil War, grew rancorous and contagious. It led to civil war. Travellers, planters, fugitive slaves, abolitionists, and other interested parties had strong opinions about slavery which informed their testimony. Historians, therefore, must consider carefully the author's motives and interests as they weigh the value of each contemporary record on slavery.

Whatever the effects of the slavery controversy on the veracity of contemporary accounts, the consuming interest in the slavery question in the antebellum period brought forth a rich lode of new material. Local pride, self-defense or attack, or just plain curiosity spurred southern whites to observe the slaves more closely and to record their utterances, their folklore, and their music, as well as describe their crafts and costume. For obviously different reasons, abolitionists interviewed ex-slaves to get the slave-side rendition of bondage; indeed, such accounts became big guns in the antislavery arsenal. Along with personal narratives, or autobiographies, by former slaves, the abolitionists and other friends of blacks gathered up a huge store of riddles, folktales, stories, and music from the blacks. Such sources have their limitations; like all historical evidence, the record is partial and incomplete. The collectors lacked system, and the narrators sometimes lacked confidence. Even in their tales and spirituals, the slaves did not tell all and listeners were not sensitive enough to understand all. By the twentieth century, when the collection of folklore and ex-slave narratives was more systematic, memories had blurred and black folklore had been filtered through the experience of freedom. Folklore and memory, after all, are not static, and as Charles Joyner shows in his essay, folk culture varies according to time *and* place.

Still, the non-literary evidence for the first time promised an entrance into the interior world of the slaves. It was evidence that the slaves created for themselves. As Gladys-Marie Fry and Lawrence Levine point out, the process of creating a folk tradition was, of itself, an affirmation of a vibrant cultural and community life among the slaves.

Today, historians, anthropologists, and sociologists have enlarged the pool of evidence available to study slavery. Thomas Webber and Charles Joyner illustrate how slave culture revealed itself in other ways than oral tradition. Games, costume, food, craftsmanship, work patterns, architecture, language, to name several "sources," all mirrored slaves' cultural and social values and organization. Apparently, the old saws that clothes make the man and you are what you eat have some validity. Significantly, much of this evidence is neutral in that it was recorded by individuals, black and white, without regard to the slavery controversy. It was difficult to impute any political meaning to the clothes slaves wore, or the games slave children played, or the way they prepared their food. Visitors to the South, Southerners, and blacks all were fascinated by the way slaves lived and recorded randomly their observations. Whatever their purposes, their records show that the slaves lived in groups and dressed, talked, ate, worked, and played differently than did most whites.

What the non-literary evidence shows is that the slaves were not compliant, passive beings wholly under the domination of their masters. Historian Stanley Elkins once argued that the fear of arbitrary punishment and the lack of any hope of escape among plantation slaves, like the inmates of Adolf Hitler's concentration camps, destroyed the slave's personality. The slave became a Sambo—childlike, irresponsible, submissive, stripped of any distinctive culture or identity, who, as a consequence, developed a degrading identity with the master. Elkins' thesis underwent withering criticism from historians and no longer holds sway, but it did raise the fundamental question of what slavery did to the slaves. The authors in this book were among the first wave of attackers who demolished Elkins' thesis, and their work here summarizes some of their important points in that debate. They showed, and in this book show, that the Sambo response to bondage was largely a role played by slaves to keep the whip off their backs and to keep the master out of their social lives as much as possible. The question remains, of course, as to how successful the slaves were in all this and as to the kind of lives they built apart from the master.

The slaves saved themselves from becoming Sambos by establishing a slave community based on an Afro-American culture. The question of African cultural survivals once wracked scholars, most of whom accepted E. Franklin Frazier's formulations that slaves lost most of their African culture in North America as they adjusted to a new social environment. But recent research, as represented in this book, unearthed strong examples of African influence among southern slaves. Wood used material culture and crafts, Genovese and Blassingame slave narratives and oral tradition, Levine songs, Gutman kinship patterns, Fry stories, Webber games, and Joyner language, dress, food, and material culture—all to make one critical point: the slaves created their own Afro-American culture and community. The issue became not one of the persistence, or purity, of African cultural forms and patterns, for in the New World where many cultures came together no culture could escape some kind of adaptation and synthesis; rather, the issue became how the Afro-American culture formed a slave community, or consensus about life, which preserved among slaves, and after emancipation blacks, a separate sense of identity, pride, and destiny. This issue runs as a leitmotif through all the essays in this book.

The crucible of Afro-American culture was religion. For many years, historians supposed that slaves had little meaningful religious life. Their arguments went something like this: Formal religion in the South was an instrument of slave control, and slave religion, such as it was, was derivative and flaccid. To be sure, religion provided a psychological catharsis of sorts for slaves as they "shouted" and sang, but the blacks' excessive emotional displays testified to a want of theological substance or direction. The slaves seemingly consoled themselves that their release from slavery's torments would come in the next world, not this one. In recent years, scholars such as Eugene Genovese and Lawrence Levine, among others, have blasted this flat construction of slave religion. By looking at religion from the slaves' perspective, or as Lawrence Levine demonstrates in his essay by listening to the plaintive spirituals and not just hearing them for example, they have discovered a dynamic, syncretic Afro-Protestantism in the Old South. It was a faith at once imbued with African conceptions of time and order, in which there was no distinction between sacred and profane or past and present, and Christian apocalyptic messages of deliverance and judgment. Conjurors, exhorters, and black preachers vied for power among the slaves but collectively challenged the master's religious authority. Meeting in groves and hollows, the slaves nurtured a religion which separated them physically and spiritually from the whites and gave them their own leaders and standards of morality. Slave religion could produce contradictory behavior, inspiring a Nat Turner as well as justifying an Uncle Tom, but in the end it was subversive, for it encouraged slaves to ponder their human condition, to think for themselves.

The family was the basic social unit of the plantation and the slave community. Masters, in their possessive, paternalistic, and self-deluding way, referred to their slaves as part of their "plantation family." The slaves were less generous. *Their* families were black alone. Until recently, few historians would concede that slaves had any family life to speak of. Historians described the slave family as fragmented and fragile at best, and social scientists generally attributed the high proportion of female-headed families among urban blacks in the twentieth century to slavery's baneful effects. Such scholars advanced the following arguments: Slave marriages lacked legal status, slave families suffered disruption from slave sales and the masters' sexual exploitation of slave women, and slave fathers exercised no real parental role as providers and protectors. Masters suffered slave families to exist, but they subjected them to so many pressures that they rarely did survive intact. Lacking the anchor of stable family life, slaves drifted morally and socially. Slavery, then, bequeathed to blacks a legacy of one-parent, unstable "family" arrangements. Slavery thrived on black submission. A viable family life requires social assertion. By using slave sources and adopting the slaves' angle of vision to assess the institution, historians now find abundant evidence of such assertion. Powerful kinship ties and a remarkably resilient family structure grew up in bondage and gave the slaves a sense of community and order.

Some demographic facts offer the first clues to the slave family's survival. Almost all slaves in the Old South were born in America. For political and humanitarian reasons, the founding fathers closed the African slave trade to the United States by 1808; consequently, American slaveholders relied on the natural increase of slaves to keep pace with the rising demand for slave labor in the antebellum South. It behooved the master to encourage family life among the slaves. Stable families meant more slaves, and so, more wealth for the masters. For whatever reasons, slaves reproduced to increase the American slave population substantially; indeed, the slaves of the South were the only significant New World slave population to reproduce themselves. Settling slaves by family also served as a social control device. The threat of sale or punishment of a family member was a powerful weapon for masters. The wails of mothers losing children on the auction block and, after emancipation, the freedmen's search for lost relatives bore grim witness to the slaveholders' power. But there were some restraints on the master, as Eugene Genovese suggests. A master who disrupted a slave family invited revenge and disorder. Then, too, masters who talked much about their slaves being part of "their family" and who subscribed to Victorian morality were probably a little squeamish about breaking up slave families by sale or assaulting slave women sexually. They did those things—and to a surprising degree argues Herbert Gutman—but they risked reprisals in doing so.

Many historians now believe that slaves redefined family life to suit their particular condition as slaves. For example, slaves did not expect the slave father to provide all things and to protect in all ways. The slave father assumed a narrower role as provider and protector by hunting, fishing, gardening, or stealing to supplement the family's diet and by standing between bullies or even lustful whites who threatened family members. The insecurity of the nuclear family encouraged the slaves to develop an extended kin network which, because of the interstate slave trade and migration, traversed the whole South by 1860. This network provided surrogate parents and siblings when necessary, and it provided a vehicle for the transmission of Afro-American culture over time and place. The slaves' close attention to choosing marriage partners, to naming children, to according respect to elders further demonstrates that slaves had clear family identities and standards of proper social behavior in families. Their decisions about courtship and social niceties gave them control over crucial areas of their social world. Looking at the last generation of slaves, Gutman finds that slaves had a history of long-lasting, stable unions whenever masters did not intrude into family life. Scholars are unsure whether the slave family represents a continuation of African patterns or a product of the American environment, or both, but few scholars dispute the ability of the slave family to adapt to the vicissitudes of chattel slavery. How those adaptations affected slave culture and society, however, remain open questions.

The dissemination of Afro-American culture and the distribution of status among slaves further reveal how the slaves responded to bondage. Socialization of slaves began early, as Gladys-Marie Fry and Thomas Webber demonstrate. By the time the slaves went to work in the fields, they had formed the basic social relationships and values about religion, family, and community that would govern their lives thereafter. Slave children were immersed deeply into Afro-American culture, and through this process into the slave community, through a steady regimen of stories, parental guidance, and games. The high status of religious figures, elders, teachers, storytellers, and resistors in the slave community gauges the slaves' values. According to John Blassingame, slaves trusted and revered 1) those who were the farthest removed from the master's interest and least beholden to him and 2) those slaves who preserved Afro-American culture. In effect, slaves wanted to be the arbiters of their own society, and they wanted to keep alive their distinct culture because it was their own.

Through ceremony, costume, and crafts, folklore, food, and family, through music, language, so many ways, the slaves struggled to ward off the debasement and self-condemnation that chattel slavery encouraged. They tried to build a cultural and social community in the slave quarters to prevent social, psychological, and cultural chaos in their lives. The dynamics and the success of that struggle are the principal concerns of this book.

Part I

The Seeds of Slavery
and
The Slave Community

"It was a Negro Taught Them",
A New Look at African Labor in Early South Carolina

PETER H. WOOD

In this essay Peter H. Wood offers a thesis about cultural survival and adaptation among enslaved Africans in early South Carolina—an argument he developed more fully in his influential book, *Black Majority: Negroes in South Carolina from 1670 Through the Stono Rebellion* (1974). Wood describes the enslaved Africans' comparative advantages over Europeans in technical skills appropriate to the semi-tropical environment of South Carolina. Such skills allowed the Africans to adapt to South Carolina with less cultural disruption than many early European settlers there and to infuse African culture into white settler society. Acculturation was a two-way street. Ironically, hints Wood, the Africans' adaptability made them valuable, and therefore more attractive, as slaves but also provided them with the means of resisting their masters. What does the "easy" transfer of African patterns of work and craftsmanship to colonial South Carolina suggest about the social effects of enslavement and removal of Africans to the New World? How did the slaves' technical skills and adaptation to the South Carolina environment hasten, or retard, their acculturation? In what ways might the retention of African skills and traditions contribute to

Reprinted from Peter H. Wood, " 'It was a Negro Taught Them,' A New Look at African Labor in Early South Carolina," in Roger D. Abrahams and John F. Szwed, editors, *Discovering Afro-America* (Leiden: E.J. Brill, 1975), pp. 26-42, without notes, by the permission of the publisher.

an Afro-American identity among the slaves? What was the white settlers' response to the Africans' skills and customs? Compare Wood's arguments about acculturation and work with those of Gerald Mullin in the next selection.

When Col. John Barnwell of South Carolina laid siege to the stronghold of the Tuscarora Indians in the spring of 1712, he noticed a special ingenuity in the fortification. "I immediately viewed the Fort with a prospective glass and found it strong," the commander wrote. Not only were there impressive trenches, bastions, and earthworks to ward off attack, but heavy tree limbs had been placed around the fort making any approach difficult and hiding innumerable "large reeds & canes to run into the people's legs." What struck Barnwell particularly was the fact that, according to the fort's occupants, "it was a runaway negro taught them to fortify thus." At that early date blacks and whites had lived in the region for scarcely a generation, and it is not likely that this slave, identified only as "Harry," had been born in Carolina. Instead it seems probable that he had grown up in Africa and had lived in South Carolina before he was "sold into Virginia for roguery & . . . fled to the Tuscaruros." If Harry's African know-how caught the South Carolina commander off guard, it may also startle modern historians, for this obscure incident exemplifies an intriguing aspect of Afro-American history which has not yet been adequately explored.

Colonial South Carolina is an excellent place to begin searching the cultural baggage of early black immigrants for what anthropologists have termed "carryovers". More slaves entered North America through Charleston (called Charlestown until 1783) than through any other single port, and no other mainland region had so high a ratio of Africans to Europeans throughout the eighteenth century as did South Carolina. Early migrants from Barbados and other places where black slavery was well-established brought Negro workers with them when they could afford it. In the initial years after 1670, however, most English settlers hoped to meet the colony's intensive labor needs in other ways. Attempts were made to procure a steady supply of European workers and to employ neighboring Indians on a regular basis, but neither of these sources could meet the demand. Within half a century Negroes constituted a majority of the settlement's population, and additional black slaves were being imported regularly from Africa.

That such a large percentage of early South Carolinians were Negroes has never been thoroughly explained, though basic contributing factors have long been recognized: European racism, colonial precedent, and the proximity of the African trading routes. No other workers were available for such extended terms, in such large numbers, at so low a rate. Indeed, such slave labor was so has always seemed almost inevitable. And perhaps for this very reason, the question of whether Negroes brought with them any inherited knowledge and practical skills from the African continent has seemed irrelevant to white historians. Though the anthropologist Melville Herskovits challenged "The Myth of the Negro Past" more than thirty years ago, the American historian has tended to uphold the legend that blacks had no prior cultures of any consequence, or that if they did, little could have survived the traumatic Middle Passage. . . . Africans, according to this approach, were imported *in spite* of being thoroughly unskilled (or perhaps in part *because* of it). And it followed from this that the central chore which faced European masters was one of patient and one-sided education, so that "ignorant" slaves could be taught to manage simple tasks.

Yet, in actuality something very different seems to have taken place. In the earliest years of colonization slaves who had passed through the Creole culture of the West Indies demonstrated unsuspected talents. Within several decades the necessity for labor of any sort led to an increase in the size and diversity of the Negro population, and a further variety of African skills emerged which were strikingly appropriate to the lowland frontier. Slaves, therefore, were far from being the passive objects of white instruction. A process of mutual education took place among the slaves themselves, despite initial language problems. And many of these workers, regardless of legal status, occasionally ended up teaching their masters. Africans, as will be made clear, sometimes proved knowledgeable and competent in areas where Europeans remained disdainful or ignorant. Hence the problem faced by white Carolinians during the first and second generations of settlement was less one of imparting knowledge to unskilled workers than of controlling for their own ends black expertise which could, as in Harry's case, be readily turned against them.

Though hitherto unacknowledged, the comparative advantages which Africans possessed over Europeans in this New World setting can be seen in a variety of different ways. South Carolina, first of all, was in a different geographic zone from England and from all the earlier English colonies in mainland North America. This fact was pleasing to white settlers on one level, but disconcerting on another, and they were slow to make the adjustments necessary for life in a somewhat alien semi-tropical region. John Lawson, an amateur naturalist who explored the Carolinas at the start of the eighteenth century, commented that if English colonists "would be so curious as to make nice Observations of the Soil, and other remarkable Accidents, they would soon be acquainted with the Nature of the Earth and Climate, and be better qualified to manage their Agriculture to more Certainty." But he went on to admit, as would Jefferson and others after him, that Europeans seemed to become less careful and observant rather than more so in the unfamiliar environment of the American South.

West Africans, on the other hand, were not only more accustomed to the flora and fauna of the subtropical climate generally, but they possessed an orientation toward what Levi-Strauss has called "extreme familiarity with the biological environment, . . . passionate attention . . . to it and . . . precise knowledge of it." Even prior to the 1600's black slaves had established a reputation for being able to subsist off the land more readily than Europeans in the Southeast. . . . In Carolina their ability to cope with this particular natural world was demonstrated, and reinforced, by the reliance Europeans put upon them to fend for themselves and others. Instances of black self-sufficiency (like instances of Indian assistance) made a lasting impression upon less well acclimated whites, and as late as 1775 we find an influential English text repeating the doctrine that in Carolina, "The common idea . . . is, that one Indian, or dextrous negroe, will, with his gun and netts, get as much game and fish as five families can eat; and the slaves support themselves in provisions, besides raising . . . staples."

By far the largest number of peope entering South Carolina during the colonial period came from West Africa, and, in the course of a century of immigration, items indigenous to parts of that vast region were transported with them. For example, though white colonists would debate at length which European should receive credit for introducing the first bag of rice seed, it is possible that successful rice cultivation, to be discussed separately later, followed the arrival of seeds aboard a ship from Africa. Often the botanical imprecision of contemporary Englishmen makes it hard to say exactly which plants were introduced and when. Semantic confusion about Guinea corn and Indian corn provides a case in point. Maurice Mathews reported during the initial summer of settlement that along with Indian corn, "Guiney Corne growes very well here, but this being ye first I euer planted ye perfection I will not Aver till ye Winter doth come in." This grain or some subsequent variety clearly took hold, for in the next generation Lawson reported Guinea corn to be thriving; he noted it was used mostly for hogs, and poultry, while adding that many black slaves ate "nothing but" Indian corn (with salt). . . .

The West African and Carolinian climates were similar enough so that even where flora and fauna were not literally transplanted, a great deal of knowledge proved transferable. African cultures placed high priority on their extensive pharmacopoeia, and details known through oral tradition were readily transported to the New World. For example, expertise included familiarity with a variety of herbal antidotes and abortives. . . . Although certain medicinal knowledge was confined to specially experienced slaves (some of whom were known openly as "doctors"), almost all blacks showed a general familiarity with lowland plants. Negroes regularly gathered berries and wild herbs for their own use and for sale. John Brickell noted of slaves in Carolina, for example, that "on Sundays, they gather Snake-Root, otherwise it would be excessive dear if the Christians were to gather it." The economic benefits to be derived from workers with such horticultural skills were not lost upon speculative Europeans. . . .

Bringing a greater awareness of the environment with them, foreign slaves were better able to profit from contact with native Indians than were their equally foreign masters. A variety of plants and processes were known to both West African and southeastern American cultures, and such knowledge must have been shared and reinforced upon contact. Gourds, for example, served as milk pails along the Gambia River in much the same way calabashes had long provided water buckets beside the Ashley. The creation of elaborate baskets, boxes, and mats from various reeds and grasses was familiar to both black and red, and South Carolina's strong basket-weaving tradition, still plainly visible on the roadsides north of Charleston, undoubtedly represents an early fusion of Negro and Indian skills. . . .

Through the first two generations of settlement Indians were common among the Negroes in lowland Carolina, both as fellow slaves and as free neighbors. But the number of Indians steadily declined, and as their once-formidable know-how dissipated it was the Negroes who assimilated the largest share of their lore and who increasingly took over their responsibilites as "pathfinders" in the Southern wilderness. Blacks became responsible for transporting goods to market by land and water and for ferrying passengers and livestock. From the first years of settlement the primary means of direct communication between masters was through letters carried by slaves. . . .

There is no better illustration of white reliance upon black knowledge of the environment than the fact that slaves became quite literally the guides of their masters. Contemporary records give adequate testimony. John Lawson, travelling from the Ashley to the Santee by canoe at the start of the eighteenth century, relates that at one point a local doctor "sent his Negro to guide us over the Head of the Swamp." A public official such as the Provost Marshal would sometimes be loaned a slave boy "to Show him the way" between plantations. . . .

It is striking to find black familiarity with the land more than matched by familiarity with the coastal sea. Although Europeans were unrivaled as the builders and navigators of oceangoing ships, there was little in the background of most white immigrants to prepare them for negotiating the labyrinth of unchanneled swamps and tidal marshes which interlaced the lowland settlement. Afro-Americans drew on a different heritage. Some slaves had scarcely seen deep water before their forced passage to America, and none had sailed in ocean vessels; yet many had grown up along rivers or beside the ocean and were far more at home in this element than most Europeans, for whom a simple bath was still exceptional. . . . Most importantly, a large number of slaves were more at home than their masters in dugout canoes, and these slender boats were the central means of transportation in South Carolina for several generations while roads and bridges were still too poor and infrequent for easy land travel. Small canoes were hollowed from single cypress logs by Negroes or Indians, or by whites whom they instructed in the craft. . . .

In South Carolina slave men were often advertised in terms of their abilities on the water: "a very good Sailor, and used for 5 years to row in Boats, . . . a Lad chiefly used to row in Boats," "a fine strong Negro Man, that has been used to the Sea, which he is very fit for, or to go in a Pettiaugua," "all fine Fellows in Boats or Pettiau's." So many Negroes brought these skills with them, or learned their seamanship in the colony from other slaves, that black familiarity with boating was accepted as axiomatic among whites. In 1741, when Henry Bedon advertised two Negro men "capable to go in a Pettiauger" who had been "going by the Water above 10 Years," he added that the pair "understands their Business as well as most of their Colour." "Their business" often included fishing, and it is not surprising that in the West Indian and southern colonies Africans quickly proved able to supply both themselves and their European owners with fish. In Charleston, an entire class of "fishing Negroes" had emerged early in the eighteenth century, replacing local Indians as masters of the plentiful waters. . . .

Skill with hooks and harpoons was complemented by other techniques more common in Africa and the Caribbean than in Europe. The poisoning of streams to catch fish was known in West Africa, and fish drugging was also practised in the West Indies, first by Island Caribs and later by Negro slaves. They dammed up a stream or inlet and added an intoxicating mixture of quicklime and plant juices to the water. They could then gather inebriated but edible fish from the pool almost at will. Inhabitants of South Carolina in the early eighteenth century exploited a similar tactic, for in 1726 the Assembly charged that "many persons in this Province do often use the pernicious practice of poisoning the creeks in order to catch great quantity of fish," and a public whipping was imposed upon any slave convicted of the act.

West African Negroes may also have imported the art of net casting, which became an established tradition in the tidal shallows of Carolina. The doctor aboard an American slaving vessel off the Gold Coast in the mid-eighteenth century recorded in his journal: "It is impossible to imagine how very dextrous the negroes are in catching fish with a net, this morning I watch'd one man throw one of 3 yards deep, and hale it in himself with innumerable fish." Weighted drawstring nets, like the dugout canoes from which they were cast, may have represented the syncretic blend of several ancient Atlantic fishing traditions. The men who could handle nets could also mend them; in 1737 a runaway named Moses was reported to be "well known in Charlestown, having been a Fisherman there for some time, & hath been often employed in knitting of Nets." The prevalence of Negro commercial fishermen in the Southeast, as in the Caribbean, continued long after the end of slavery, and blacks who man shrimpboats in present-day Carolina earn their living at a calling familiar to many of their West African forebears.

No single industry was more important to the early settlement in South Carolina than the raising of livestock. While the first generation of Englishmen experimented unsuccessfully with such strange crops as grapes, olives, cotton, rice, indigo, and ginger in the hopes of finding an appropriate staple, their livelihood depended in large measure upon the cattle and hogs that could be raised with a minimum of labor. Beef and pork were in great demand in the West Indies, and these at least were items which the English had long produced. But even here there was an unfamiliar element. According to traditional European patterns of animal husbandry, farmers confined their cows in pastures, milked them regularly, and slaughtered them annually. Since winter fodder was limited, Europeans maintained only enough stock through the cold months to replenish their herds in the following spring. This practice made little sense in a region where cattle could "feed themselves perfectly well at no cost whatever" throughout the year. Stock grew lean, but rarely starved in South Carolina's mild winters. Colonists therefore might build up large herds with little effort, a fact which could benefit the settlement but which dismayed the Proprietors in London. It has been "our designe", they stated indignantly, "to have Planters there and not Graziers."

Africans, however, had no such disdain for open grazing, and many of the slaves entering South Carolina after 1670 may have had experience in tending large herds. Melville Herskovits, along with others, has pointed out that although domesticated cattle were absent from the Congo region due to the presence of the tsetse fly, such animals were common along much of the African coast to the north and west. Stock was even traded for export on occasion. . . .

As early as the 1670's there is evidence of absentee investors relying upon Negro slaves to develop herds of cattle in Carolina. Even when the white owner lived within the province, the care of his livestock often fell to a black. The slave would build a small "cowpen" in some remote region, attend the calves and guard the grazing stock at night. . . .

At first the Carolina settlement occupied a doubly colonial status, struggling to supply provisions to other English colonies. The development of a trade in naval stores soon enabled the settlement to become a staple producer in its own right, but it was the cultivation of rice as an export commodity which came to dominate Carolina life in the course of the eighteenth century. Despite its eventual prominence, the mastery of this grain took more than a generation, for rice was a crop about which Englishmen, even those who had lived in the Caribbean, knew nothing at all. White immigrants from elsewhere in northern Europe were equally ignorant, and local Indians who gathered small quantities of wild rice had little to teach them. . . . In contrast to Europeans, Negroes from the West Coast of Africa were widely familiar with rice planting. Those Africans who were accustomed to growing rice on one side of the Atlantic, and who found themselves raising the same crop on the other side, did not markedly alter their annual routine. When New World slaves planted rice in the spring by pressing a hole with the heel and covering the seeds with the foot, the motion used was demonstrably similiar to that employed in West Africa. In summer, when Carolina blacks moved through the rice fields in a row, hoeing in unison to work songs, the pattern of cultivation was not one imposed by European owners but rather one retained from West African forebears. And in October, when the threshed grain was "fanned" in the wind, the wide flat winnowing basket was made by black hands after an African design.

Those familiar with growing and harvesting rice must also have known how to process it, so it is interesting to speculate about the origins of the mortar and pestle technique which became the accepted method for removing rice grains from their husks. Efforts by Europeans to develop alternative "engines" proved of no avail, and this process remained the most efficient way to "clean" the rice crop throughout the colonial period. Since some form of the mortar and pestle is familiar to agricultural peoples throughout the world, a variety of possible (and impossible) sources have been suggested for this device. But the most logical origin for this technique is the coast of Africa, for there was a strikingly close resemblance between the traditional West African means of pounding rice and the process used by slaves in South Carolina. Several Negroes, usually women, cleaned the grain a small amount at a time by putting it in a wooden mortar which was hollowed from the upright trunk of a pine or cypress. It was beaten with long wooden pestles which had a sharp edge at one end for removing the husks and a flat tip at the other for whitening the grains. Even the songs sung by the slaves who threshed and pounded the rice may have retained African elements.

In the establishment of rice cultivation, as in numerous other areas, historians have ignored the possibility that Afro-Americans could have contributed anything more than menial labor to South Carolina's early development. Yet Negro slaves, faced with limited food supplies before 1700 and encouraged to raise their own subsistence, could readily have succeeded in nurturing rice where their masters had failed. It would not have taken many such incidents to demonstrate to the anxious English that rice was a potential staple and that Africans were its most logical cultivators and processors. Some such chain of events may even have provided the background for Edward Randolph's report to the Lords of Trade in 1700 that Englishmen in Carolina had "now found out the true way of raising and husking Rice." Needless to say, by no means every slave entering South Carolina had been drawn from an African rice field, and many, perhaps even a great majority, had never seen a rice plant. But it is important to consider the fact that literally hundreds of black immigrants were more familiar with the planting, hoeing, processing, and cooking of rice than were the European settlers who purchased them.

Despite the usefulness of all such African skills to the colony's development, there existed a reverse side to the coin. While it is clear that Negro South Carolinians made early contributions to the regional culture, it is also clear that they received little recompense for their participation and that they were bound to respond to this fact. Slaves quickly proved that the same abilities which benefitted Europeans, such as gathering herbs and guiding canoes, could also be used to oppose and threaten them. . . .

Black knowledge of herbs and poisons was the most vivid reminder that Negro expertise could be a two-edged sword. In West Africa, the obeah-men and others with herbal know-how to combat poisoning could inflict it as well, and this gave slaves a weapon against their new white masters. In Jamacia, poisoning was a commonplace means of black resistance in the eighteenth century, and incidents were also familiar in the mainland colonies. In South Carolina the administering of poison by a slave was made a felony in the stiff Negro Act of 1740 which followed in the wake of the Stono Rebellion. Eleven years later an additional law was written, stating that "the detestable crime of poisoning hath of late been frequently committed by many slaves in this Province, and notwithstanding the execution of several criminals for that offence, yet it has not been sufficient to deter others from being guilty of the same."

The statute of 1751 suggests the seriousness with which white legislators viewed the poisoning threat, for they attempted belatedly to root out longstanding Negro knowledge and the administration of medicinal drugs. . . . Yet even this strict legislation was apparently not enough to suppress such resistance, for in 1761 the *Gazette* reported that "The negroes have again begun the hellish practice of poisonings.". . .

Europeans entering South Carolina did not anticipate black skills or the uses to which they might be put. Indeed, most were ignorant of the environment they entered and of the labor they purchased. But white settlers soon realized that African workers possessed expertise which could be exploited and knowledge which was to be feared. Within several generations, the Europeans had imparted aspects of their culture to the slaves and had themselves acquired practical knowledge in matters such as ricegrowing. Consequently, Negro skills rapidly lost distinctiveness during the middle decades of the eighteenth century. By that time, however, black South Carolinians had already contributed significantly to the colony's initial growth, and ironically these early contributions, although threatening at times, served to strengthen rather than to weaken the European rationale for perpetuating an African labor force. A full generation before the American Revolution, race slavery had become a firmly established institution in the region and white patterns of exploitation and fear were destined to run their lengthy course.

Rethinking American Negro Slavery
From the Vantage Point
of the Colonial Era

GERALD W. MULLIN

Gerald (Michael) W. Mullin is the author of *Flight and Rebellion: Slave Resistance in Eighteenth-Century Virginia* (1972), a seminal study of acculturation and assimilation among enslaved Africans and the roots of Afro-American community life. In this selection Mullin shows that slavery was not a static social or economic institution. He traces slavery's evolution from its seigneurial model in colonial America to its capitalistic form in the Old South. He notes different acculturation experiences of enslaved Africans in Virginia and South Carolina. How did changes in plantation operations affect the slaves' work, community life, and sense of individuality? How did the slaves' acculturation influence the organization of the plantation? Compare Mullin's arguments about acculturation with those of Wood in the previous essay. Mullin also introduces the master as an important socializing force in American slave society. In what ways did relations between master and slave change as the nature of plantation organization and the acculturation of slaves changed over time? How did the presence

Reprinted from Gerald W. Mullin, "Rethinking American Negro Slavery from the Vantage Point of the Colonial Era," *Louisiana Studies: An Interdisciplinary Journal of the South*, XII (Summer, 1973), pp. 398, 404-413, 415-422, without notes, by permission of the Managing Editor.

of planters living among the slaves on the plantations promote the slaves' acculturation? Compare Mullin's arguments about plantation organization and planter paternalism in the Old South with those of Eugene Genovese in the next selection.

A surge of interest in Afro-American history has pushed to the fore a familiar and important controversy—the relationship between ante-bellum society and its most distinctive institution, the plantation. Generally historians have construed the plantation either as a kind of seignorial manor and the planter's way of life, or as a factory in the field and simply the planter's business. Constructions of this weight require a solid foundation, but scholars who have used the plantation as little more than a literary device, a metaphor for Southern values and ways, have not built well.

The plantation would be a more reliable guide to Southern society if we saw it from microcosmic, long-range, and comparative perspectives, which clarified the perameters—regional variations in settlement patterns and crops—as well as the center, the relationships among the institution's major components—organization, work routines, and the roles of planter, overseer, and slave. Most important, an effective model of the plantation would show the connections between institution and society, and indicate how historical change for one component influenced the development of the others.

This arduous but rewarding task cannot be done here in an exploratory essay about plantation organization, and the planter's role (an invaluable way of linking the institution to society and to major historical developments), as they changed through time. To do this requires that a sharper distinction be made between colonial and ante-bellum plantations, and that attention be shifted both from the drama of sectional conflict to the humdrum reality of plantation routines, and from the master class to those blacks and whites whose everyday, ordinary existences were massively and profoundly influenced by the structures and rhythms of staple production. . . .

Slavery in the colonial era was not simply a prelude to ante-bellum slavery. In the eighteenth century, particularly, its uniqueness stemmed from a process that had passed from the scene by 1800: the first stirrings of an American nationalism,—eventually of revolutionary dimensions that was shaped by the coming of age of the only landed aristocracy in America: and Africans, who slowly became Negroes as they changed their Old World customs and adjusted to the cruel realities of plantation slavery. A view of these distinctive attributes, from one eighteenth-century slave society in which planters saw Africans as peasants and themselves as manor lords with a civilizing mission, is provided by a boastful letter from a wealthy tobacco planter to an English earl:

> Besides the advantage of a pure Air, we abound in all kinds of Provisions without expense (I mean we who have Plantations). I have a large family of my own. . . . Like one of the Patriachs, I have my Flocks and my Herds, my Bond-men and Bond-women, and every Soart of Trade amongst my own Servants, so that I live in a kind of Independence on every one but Providence. However this Soart of Life is without expense, yet it is attended with a great deal of trouble. I must take care to keep all my people to their Duty, to set all the Springs in motion. . . . But then 'tis an amusement in this silent Country and a continual exercise of our Patience and Economy.
>
> Another thing My Lord that recommends this Country very much— we sit securely under our vines and our fig trees without any danger to our property. . . . [Although] we have often needy Governors, and pilfering convicts sent among us.

William Byrd's paternalistic attitudes and feudal images are deceptive. For in his or any colonial setting 'sitting securely under vines and fig trees' was largely wishful thinking. Forced to deal with circumstances unknown to their nineteenth-century counterparts, Byrd and his countrymen talked about patriarchal independence, when in reality they were destined to be colonial planters and slaveowners in a mercantilist Empire: as colonists they were obliged to recognize that authority for the most important decisions for their country originated outside its boundaries in England. As planters they had to submit to the Mother Country's control of manufactured goods, credit arrangements and prices, and as slaveowners, they exploited Africa as a cheap and consistent source of labor, only to gradually realize how thoroughly dependent they were on slaves.

Byrd's idyll was defined by space as well as time. In the midst of British officials and Africans at various stages of socialization, slaveowners expressed a need to be free in ways best suited to their local topographic, demographic and urban conditions. In the tobacco colonies an extensive network of navigable rivers, a chronic absence of town life, and the gentry's ambition to be "independent on Every one but Providence," scattered settlers far into the interior of the country where they built the large and comparatively self-sufficient plantations that were the focus of their lives. Determined to be autonomous tobacco planters encouraged cultural change among slaves, because their tanneries, blacksmith and carpentry shops required literate, skilled artisans. In Virginia, the oldest area of permanent settlement in British America, "living bravely," on autarkic, self-contained, plantations maintained by black craftsmen, was an old, resilient tradition stemming from the settlers' Elizabethan origins. . . .

Colonial Virginia . . . was . . . a premodern society—small-scale, corporate, God-fearing and deferential, in which slave-owners were paternalistic and plantations were manors, "little Fortress[es] of Independency"—that is, once they came to be economically self-sufficient and diversified, as Africans (or usually their American-born children) were assimilated and trained as artisans. In these circumstances then the tobacco gentry's patriarchal model for plantation organization was clearly a reaction to a particular time and place.

In the rice-growing region of South Carolina, however, settled more than fifty years later by Barbadians and Englishmen of the Restoration Era, a different kind of river system, a much higher percentage of unacculturated and untrained Africans among all slaves, and one of the largest cities in colonial America produced different relationships between the land and its settlers. The low country planters, concentrated on a plain of sea islands and marsh that was extremely productive agriculturally but most unhealthy, grew only rice on specialized—not diversified—plantations, employed few black artisans, and spent much of their time in Charleston, the source of the urban goods and services that the tidewater tobacco planters had to produce on their own plantations. Rice in fact made so much more money than tobacco (the weed's market declined severely after 1750, producing a string of bankruptcies and forcing planters into wheat and general farming) that by mid-century the low country had the highest per capita income in America, and probably the fastest growth rate in the world. By the 1750s a monoculture society had developed and, in important ways, South Carolina was similar to British West Indian society: that is, a colony characterized by a well defined urban export area (and a city rather than the plantation as the focus for white society and culture), great fortunes and extensive planter absenteeism.

Further comparisons between rice and tobacco regions, as an

indication of what ante-bellum plantations changed from, should be made from the slave's vantage point. A view from the bottom up accomplishes (as it should) much more than simply a reconstruction of the lives and settings of a neglected and historically silent people. Examining the reactions of Africans illuminates a process (if shorthand is admissable) in which plantation society once small-scale, corporate and colonial came to be populous, individualistic and sovereign; and planters inclined to be paternalistic fathers became impersonal businessmen.

In the colonial era slave behavior was largely accountable to the extent of planter absenteeism, the slave's origin (birthplace), job and degree of cultural change (as seen in the most plentiful and reliable sources on slaves, those describing resistance). For our purposes, the relationships between acculturation levels and styles of resistance, on the one hand, and the planter's role, on the other, are most informative about comparisons between colonial and ante-bellum plantations.

Acculturation was the process in which native Africans, while learning English and other ways whites would have them behave, changed their customs and became Negroes. This process was marked by three stages, and often lasted more than a generation (especially in South Carolina). Native Africans (referred to as "outlandish"), at the first level of socialization, seldom learned English well, nor lost the essentials of an African orientation. When forced into field labor, they were called "new Negroes," a second stage of acculturation; and, as they began the slow, and sometimes demoralizing process of cultural change, their reactions were dramatically transformed into individualistic rather than collective patterns.

Philosophically as well as socially Africans were aliens, whose acts of rebellion often exposed novel preconceptions and expectations about relations with others and the way the world worked. As a communal and tribal folk, they saw slavery as a temporary misfortune, to be confronted cooperatively, and rejected totally. In the colonial period Africans were the only slaves reported as runaways in large groups who often traveled into the wilds, where they attempted to reestablish village life as they knew it before they were enslaved. But assimilated blacks (especially artisans), the third level of acculturation, typically resisted slavery alone, and in ways that were not nearly as threatening to the slave system. They ran off and often hired themselves out in cities, where in a labor starved economy talented runaways (white servants as well as slaves) often achieved a modicum of freedom, which was impossible within the confines of the plantation.

The concept of cultural change dramatizes the historical dimension of slavery, while providing a more precise way of talking about slave behavior. But "acculturation" is a rather stilted, dormant word, which does not begin to convey a sense of the tragic confrontation among races in colonial America. The epic European conquest, settlement, and importation of Africans (which brought nearly 200,000 slaves to the eighteenth-century mainland) set in motion massive but often intimate, encounters between blacks and whites, that profoundly shaped our basic cultural modalities (sex, diet, domesticity, language, politics and religion) in ways that are still only little understood.

Documents about Africans in South Carolina are most informative about the unique mood and feeling of colonial slavery. In the Carolina low country slaves in organized, war-like groups, often fled to the frontier, the Spanish presidio at St. Augustine, Florida; or, rebelled and fought back.

In September 1739 Angolans, who were part of a large and poorly supervised road crew on the Stono River, led one of the largest slave uprisings ever in North America. Although Africans were usually as competent as Indians in surviving in the wilderness, they were occasionally confused by their isolation on the rice plantations, as well as their rapid movement from a west to an east coast, which distorted ways of making the world intelligible (by calculating direction and time). The Stono insurrectionists were no exception. After burning several plantations and killing a score of whites, Sunday night, September 9, their force grew rapidly from twenty to sixty, "some say a Hundred," by additions of "new Negroes." Monday morning they "burnt all before them without Opposition," swept south and west through the hamlet of Jacksonboro; and, later in the day, "thinking they were now victorious over the whole Province," they halted in a field, and set to Dancing, Singing and beating Drums, to draw more Negroes to them." But the Africans had marched only ten miles to the Pon Pon River, where they were eventually surrounded, scattered or shot. The rebellion ended after the murder of twenty-one whites and more than forty blacks, but two years later Settlement Indians were still presenting claims to the legislature for rebels whom they had tracked down and killed.

These violent rituals of a society groping toward basic arrangements between races rarely occurred after 1750. Acculturation, which diffused black anger by making slaves less cooperative, proceeded rapidly. And by the end of the slave trade in 1807, "White Over Black," already an intrinsic part of what it meant to be an American in the New Nation, was also largely an uncontested reality.

The extent and quality of planter absenteeism—how slave-owners executed the role of master—was another major variable determining slave behavior. Absenteeism was not so much a question of whether or not an owner lived at home; but rather, the degree to which the plantation was his base of operations, the way he oriented himself to the world; how much he came and went, and so, the extent to which he was personally involved in its daily supervision. Slave owners whose only home was the plantation, whose families lived amongst the artisans and household servants of the home quarter (all of whom in turn served as models of cultural change for "new Negroes"), were the real patriachs in Southern history. Their knowledge of each slave, and willingness to intervene in the blacks' domestic lives, ensured both a faster rate of assimilation and degree of compliance than those whose slaves, supervised by overseers and black drivers, lived among their own.

Africans were in part the creatures of ecological perameters and the overriding objectives of plantation production, but acculturation was a two-way street. Slaves exerted significant influence of their own, and, at a crucial moment, when planters for the first time were working out the best techniques for growing staples with slaves. In order to curb resistance (which in the colonial period was so often African—that is, persistent, organized and dangerous), planters soon realized that they must either live at home, or provide a rationalized system of rules, routine and command, a clearly perceived hierarchy of authority, as a substitute for their own constant surveillance, worrisome attention to detail, encourgement of cultural change by example, and paternalistic treatment of slaves. Eighteenth-century tobacco plantations and the larger ante-bellum enterprises best illustrate these two ways of organizing staple production for profit, status and power. The situation in South Carolina is more confusing, but suggestive, because the sources, which are so sparse and thin, offer glimpses of the more progressive managerial styles that characterized large ante-bellum plantations.

The patriarchal role—which did not survive the change from the Colonial to the Early National period—was most highly refined in the Chesapeake Bay region. Tobacco patriarchs lived on their plantations and took their fatherly roles seriously, while habitually referring to their slaves as "my people," "my Bondsmen," "the black members of my family." They saw slave rebelliousness as a transgression of the Fifth Commandment, "Honour thy Father and thy Mother," and assumed that both master and slave had certain rights and obligations: "I must again desire that you will keep Tommy strictly to his Duty & obedience"; "cruelty to the poor slaves is a thing I always Abhored. I would think myself happy could I keep them to there [sic] duty without being Obliged to correct them." Or "began this morning to enforce my resolution of correcting the drunkenes[s] in my family by an example of Nassau." Patriarchs also controlled the most important decision made for slaves—task allotment, placing them in the house, fields or workshops. They doctored blacks who were ill and as a matter of course participated in their slaves' family lives, while moving new mates to the same quarter, placing a promising child in a workshop at a parent's request and generally enforcing their moral codes on the Africans.

But the planter's execution of these considerable responsibilities was seriously impaired by a failure to achieve real self-determination in the Empire, which in a declining tobacco market sharpened his need to be a competent father, one who saw plantation authority as absolute and indivisible. Masters used trusted slaves to report directly about activities on the satellite quarters; and insisted that overseers treat slaves as they would (that is "benevolently"), while refusing to give them the means to make crops without "Driving and Storming." Consequently relations among tobacco planters, overseers and slaves were typically chaotic; and overseers were especially vulnerable to the field slaves' petty rebelliousness.

Nonetheless the tobacco planter's presence was formidable. His direct supervision of slaves and routine channeled rebelliousness into reactions that were sporadic and non-cooperative, or at worst, into such low-keyed campaigns of sabotage as stealing, tool breaking and truancy. As the Virgina slave population became comparatively assimilated by mid-century, there were virtually no African uprisings which to the end of the colonial period haunted the rice planter's imagination. In fact in Virginia slaves at the other end of the acculturation scale, the relatively advantaged artisans, were the most troublesome, first as runaways (not simply "outlying" truants) and then as insurrectionists (who organized Gabriel Prosser's conspiracy in 1800). But, in South Carolina planters concentrated their fear of black on Africans, singling out some tribesmen aboard slavers as more dangerous than others; while Virginians in the slave market were unconcerned about the 'national character' of particular tribes, since Africans were expected to become Negroes as soon as possible.

The few surviving documents about colonial rice plantations, where absenteeisim was extensive and blacks remained African longer, present a different picture of the relationship between cultural change, rebelliousness and performance of the role of planter. While examining ways of teaching Africans English so they could be more readily proselytized, a Charleston minister for the Society for the Propagation of the Gospel in Foreign Parts, momentarily looked into the heart of [a] distinctive plantation culture. What he saw was:

> a Nation within a Nation. In all Country Settlements, they [the slaves] live in contiguous Houses and often 2, 3 or 4 Famillys of them in One House.... They labour together and converse almost wholly among themselves.

The nature of absenteeism that made this cultural autonomy possible is illuminated in the Josiah Smith Junior Letterbook (1770-1775), one of the few records of a colonial rice plantation surviving as more than a fragment. Commuting between Charleston and Georgetown (the epicenter of rice cultivation until the 1870's), Smith pursued his own business interests while managing two plantations for George Austin (once a partner with Henry Laurens in the largest slave trading company in North America), who lived in England. The tone of Smith's letters, and the patterns of authority and decision-making they reveal, were characteristically ante-bellum: the owner was non-resident, impersonal toward his slaves, and delegated authority rationally; his steward or manager visited the plantation to report on the nature of the market, and on major decisions concerning personnel, equipment and buildings. Most important, overseers and black drivers (prevalent in ante-bellum records for large plantations, but in the colonial periods mentioned only in South Carolina sources) were clearly in charge of daily activities. So the Josiah Smith Letterbook contrasts sharply with the documentation concerning the old fashioned paternalism of Chesapeake Bay society.

But tobacco planters were businesslike in their own way. Their intimate knowledge of slaves and planting was essentially the "command experience" so often cited as the basis for their ascendancy at the national level during the Revolutionary and Early National periods. Living as fathers among their black and white families, they were hard-working manor lords, who spent hours a day in the saddle, riding about the only domain in which they enjoyed real power and independence, and scrutinizing overseers, slaves, livestock and crops.... Landon Carter, one of the more scrupulous planters, even took to calculating the labor required, per plant per row, in an early time-and-motion study:

I find it wondered at how any hand can tend 28,000 corn hills planted at any distance. But surely it cannot be reasonable to do so, when it is considered that at 2 feet and 7 acre holds 3,111 corn hills and at 6 and 5 it holds only 1,452; for it is in such a case evident that at 7 and 2 the care contains more than double to what it does when planted at 6 and 5 by 202 hills. Allow then that at 6 and 5 ten thou[s] and hills only are tended; it will amount to near 7 acres that are worked each hand. Now at 7 and 3, 7 acres will contain 21,777 so that there only wants 6,223 to make up 28,000. Now that is Exactly 4 hill[s] short of 2 acres, So that the hand that tends 28,000 is only to tend 9 acres. And cannot a hand tend 9 acres of ground?

Carter's entrepreneurial instincts were shared by his fellow planters throughout British America, but kept in check while they had to be colonial patriarchs and businessmen. His methods foreshadowed a more rationalized approach to plantation organization that changed the character of master-slave relationships on large ante-bellum plantations. As agriculture became increasingly commercialized, as part of the profound changes accelerated or set in motion in the South by the Revolution, the management of slaves and plantations became less personal and more uniform and routine. . . .

The transformation in the early nineteenth-century of the social and political setting for American Negro slavery changed the planter's role and the mood of the documents he left about slavery. Planters were no longer colonists burdened by a need to make plantations self-sufficient and themselves patriarchs "independent on every one but Providence." Instead masters could be masterful in a more rational and profitable manner, by allowing the plantation to realize its potential manpower, expertise and capital in the production of staples. But as the large plantation changed from a way of life to a business, new and ominous techniques were developed for regulating and routinizing the lives of slaves.

Sensitive to the currents of the day, arbiters of the new agriculture, and publishers of the popular farm journals, demanded accountability and a systemization of production: "The plantation is a piece of machinery . . . . To operate successfully, all of its parts should be uniform and exact, and the impelling force regular and steady." "No more beautiful picture of human society can be drawn than a well orgainzed plantation. . . . A regular and systematic plan of operation of the plantation is greatly promotive of easy government. Have, therefore, all matters as far possible reduced to a system."

With the routinization of plantation operations came an even more important change: for ante-bellum slaves, most of whom lived on large plantations, slavery was no longer familial and domestic, but an impersonal and bureaucratic institution. The "Management of Negroes" articles in southern agricultural journals, written by editors, travelers, planters and overseers, encourged slaveholders to devise more effective, manipulative techniques: "Make him [the slave] as comfortable at home as possible"; "treat your negro *well* and he will respond to it with fidelity and honesty; kind words, humane consideration, justness in discipline, unhesitating authority when required, forbearance towards venal offenses, arous[e] pride of character."

Masters no longer aspired to be patriarchs but personnel managers, experts in motivational psychology: "I have found very little trouble bringing them all under my system . . . by exciting his pride I elevate the man." If slaves on Sundays insisted on dressing "in the ridiculous finery which they sometimes display, and which often provides a smile," they should not be mocked, because such dress as this "aids very materially in giving them self-respect."

The new outlook encouraged a restructuring of the plantation community. On many large units economic diversification by slave artisans (an important means of advancement for talented slaves) was all but abandoned. Aside from a household vegetable garden, a few pigs and corn fields, big plantations produced staples and little else. Most slaves were "hands" reduced to field regimens under a clearly defined chain of command—overseers, sub-overseers, drivers and foremen; and each moment of the day was as accountable and organized as the actual weighing and recording of cotton sacks at dusk. . . .

As large plantations became factories-in-the-field planters did all they could to make field workers contented charges. The antebellum counterparts—of piped-in Muzak in automobile assembly plants and lunch-hour group therapy sessions to iron-out feelings of rebelliousness in large-scale Japanese industries—were all present: slave chapels with licensed ministers; nurseries for small children whose mothers worked in the fields, and games, contests and rewards to encourage productivity and to make slavery fun. Planters large and small were quite frank about their motives for keeping slaves happy and presumably docile. But even "happiness" should be standardized. "Tattler" in the *Southern Cultivator* (November 1850) wrote: "When at work, I have no objection to their whistling or singing some lively tune, but no *drawling* tunes are allowed in the field, for their motions are almost certain to keep time with the music."

The process of making the plantation "a perfect society,"

and the worker "comfortable at home," may have cost slaves their individuality. If "Sambo" existed, that docile passive creature of the plantation's infantilizing tendencies, he was a product of the largest, late ante-bellum plantations. In the last years of slavery, rebelliousness changed, and may have decreased as a result of this tendency toward closure of the institution from all external and internal disruption: in the colonial period virtually every plantation record is filled with instances of boondoggling, feigned illness, truancy, and theft, but similar nineteenth-century records contain only rare accounts of rebellious slaves of any kind. When resistance did occur (usually on smaller, more loosely organized plantations) it was typically self-defeating, violent and often deadly.

In transforming the familial and domestic character of colonial slavery, the wealthy ante-bellum planter created an alienating world for his slaves. Herbert Marcuse tells us that "free choice among a variety of goods and services does not signify freedom if these goods and services sustain social controls over a life of toil and fear—that is, if they sustain alienation." Many slaves, reduced to mere numbers in account- and day-books were undoubtedly alienated; too enmeshed in a system with all of its small rewards to see ways out.

The new reality of plantation slavery revealed in the "Management of Negroes" articles was faithfully replicated in the records of many large plantations. In comparison with colonial crop-and day-books, entries for ante-bellum slaves were more abstract, uniform—and predictable. . . . The most astute and informative contemporary observer of ante-bellum plantation life, Frederick Law Olmsted, left this unforgettable picture of the field hands' stultifying world-of-work:

> They are constantly and steadily driven up to their work, and the stupid, plodding, machine-like manner in which they labor is painful to witness. This was especially the case with the hoe-gangs. One of them numbered nearly two hundred hands (for the force of two plantations was working together), moving across the field in parallel lines, with a considerable degree of precision. I repeatedly rode through the lines at a canter, with other horsemen, often coming upon them suddenly, without producing the smallest change or interruption in the dogged action of the laborers, or causing one of them to lift an eye from the ground.

Planter's attitudes had changed about slaves and their duties and responsibilities toward them. Their new industrial consciousness made it possible to see themselves as estate managers rather than patriarchs, and to delegate to the slave's supervisors the necessary authority to assure a smooth operation. As an effective substitute for their own constant presence on the plantation, planters established strict and comprehensive rules and regulations for overseers that dealt with all major components of the plantation operation—from the slaves' bedding, diet and housing, to the most intimate details of their religious, fraternal and family lives. Managers and overseers kept careful records of marriages, births and deaths and physician's visits, the quantities of clothing, supplies, and implements received from the planter; and quarterly inventories of stock, tools and crops, and daily accounts of cotton picked by each hand.

A quiet but significant advance in the technology of record-keeping accompanied the rationalization of plantation organization. In place of cramped and hurried notes taken in the margins or blank sheets of hand-sized almanacs, reformers like Thomas Affleck of Mississippi published detailed printed ledger pages, that brought together in one place several of the miscellaneous records usually kept by staple producers. The colonial almanacs were "comic absurdities" when compared to the new comprehensive ledgers, which Robert Williams argues were "essentially consistent with the intent and purpose of modern cost-accounting, and followed the best and most advanced principles of efficient administrative management." . . .

Paradoxically, we associate capitalistic enterprise with "Yankee ingenuity"; but trends toward strict routine and accountability were evident on southern plantations much earlier than in northern mills. This is not surprising. Planters realized that they had long controlled an indispensable factor for rationalizing such enterprises as plantations: a disciplined labor force. Slaves not only guaranteed built-in growth through their natural increase; but in slavery there were not strikes, lock-outs or even endemic turnovers of personnel. That planters enjoyed a slave's labor for a lifetime in itself probably offset the profits lost by the slaves' noncooperativeness.

Southern agricultural entrepreneurs knew what they were doing economically. Drawing upon a much longer and more consistent tradition of large-scale enterprise, with a much more disciplined and predictable labor force, than their northern counterparts, they were able sooner to get down to fundamentals: producing staples efficiently. . . .

Exceptions to this frame of reference were the small planters, who were the real patriarchs and inheritors of the paternalism that pervaded colonial slave society. Clement Eaton (in *The Growth of Southern Civilization*) introduces a typical small slaveholder, James T. Burroughs, well known as the owner of Booker T. Washington. In this family, Burroughs and his sons worked all day in the fields beside their few prime hands, and everyone ate, slept, procreated and died beneath the same roof. The letters of Rachel O'Connor, who grew cotton with sixteen slaves on Bayou Sarah, West Feliciana Parish, Louisiana, and some of Olmsted's marvelous travel reports, indicate clearly that old ways of slavery were very much alive in the ante-bellum era. But these pockets of paternalism were usually located far from the routes to market, the navigable rivers, canals and railroads. One senses that, had the Civil War not intervened, they would have been victims of an evolutionary process—reptiles in an age of mammals.

The ante-bellum South was not a semi-feudal society dominated by a class of men defending an anti-bourgeois and unprofitable way of life. From the earliest times, however, the South had been locked into the most backward sector of Old World capitalistic imperialism, the New World plantation areas. As tragic actors in this special niche, all Southerners, from the mightiest planter to the lowest slave, acquired a colonized mentality, fortified and refined by the interpersonal dynamics of the master-slave relationship. Even the application of the most advanced methods for maximizing profits from agriculture could not change that destiny. For this unhappy society civil war would be a painful but cathartic renewal.

Part II

From the Bottom Up:
Masters and Slaves,
Family and Religion

American Slaves
and
Their History

EUGENE D. GENOVESE

In his monumental book, *Roll, Jordan, Roll: The World the Slaves Made* (1974), Eugene Genovese observed that to understand the slaves it is necessary to understand the master, and vice versa. In this essay Genovese sketches the outlines of the paternalistic ethos that undergirded plantation slavery, but, more importantly, he brings slave and master together to examine their uneasy, but often intimate, relationships. In the process he redraws the slaves' portrait. Slaves are no longer victims of bondage; rather, they are creative humans who took what social space plantation paternalism offered them and used it to build the foundation of an Afro-American nation. One question rings forth from his essay: "What did the slaves do for themselves and how did they do it?" Apparently, quite a bit. Genovese uses the slaves' religion, family structure, and occupation to measure, however crudely, their social and cultural responses to bondage. Thereby, he points to new lines of inquiry about the *process* of slaves surviving as a people. Indeed, the slaves' sense of time, of moral superiority over whites, of kinship, among other things, all testified to a nascent Afro-American "nation" growing in the quarters. How did the interaction of slaves and masters determine what the slaves could do for themselves? In

From Eugene D. Genovese, "American Slaves and Their History," *The New York Review of Books*, December 3, 1970, pp. 34-43, without notes. Reprinted with permission from *The New York Review of Books*. Copyright © 1970 Nyrev, Inc.

what ways did paternalism siphon off revolutionary action by slaves, yet encourage subversive behavior? Compare Genovese's arguments about slave folk life, religion, and social structure with those of Levine, Gutman, and Blassingame in subsequent essays.

The history of the American lower classes has yet to be written. The ideological impact of the New Left, the intellectual exigencies of the black liberation movement, and the developing academic concern for the cultural aspects of politics and history have all converged to produce the expectation that this history will be written. If even a small percentage of the praise heaped upon E. P. Thompson's *The Making of the English Working Class* could be translated into an effort to extend its achievement, the future would be bright. Good work is finally being done, although little by those who periodically issue manifestoes on the need to rewrite history "from the bottom up."

History written from the bottom up is neither more nor less than history written from the top down: It is not and cannot be good history. Writing the history of a nation without considering the vicissitudes of a majority of its people is not a serious undertaking. Yet it is preposterous to suggest that there could conceivably be anything wrong with writing a book about the ruling class alone, or about one or another elite, or about any segment of society, however small. No subject is too limited to treat.

But a good historian writes well on a limited subject while taking account (if only implicitly and without a single direct reference) of the whole, whereas an inferior one confuses the need to isolate a small portion of the whole with the license to assume that that portion acted in isolation. One may, for example, write Southern history by focusing on either blacks or whites, slaves or masters, tenant farmers or landlords; but the one cannot be discussed without an understanding of the other.

The fate of master and slave was historically intertwined, and formed part of a single social process; each in his own way struggled for autonomy—struggled to end his dependence upon the other— but neither could ever wholly succeed. The first problem in the writing of social history lies in this organic antagonism: We tend to see the masters in their own terms, without acknowledging their dependence upon the slaves; but we also tend to see the slaves in the masters' terms, without acknowledging the extent to which the slaves freed themselves from domination.

There cannot be, therefore, any such thing as "history from the bottom up," but there can and should be good histories of "the bottom." A good study of plantation architecture, apart from its contribution to aesthetics, would be one that grasped the social link between the culture of the Big House and that of both the slave quarters and small nonslaveholding farm houses, for the Big House, whatever else it did, served to impress men in humble circumstances. Such a study need never mention the slave quarters or the farm houses, but if the essential insight fails or remains undeveloped and abstract, then the entire effort must remain limited. Should it succeed, then the book would be a valuable contribution to the history of Southern society and its constituent races and classes. To consider such a study "elitist" because it concerns itself with upper-class life or eschews moralistic pronouncements is a modern form of absurdity.

There is much to be said for the current notion that blacks will have to write their own history: Black people in the United States have strong claims to separate nationality, and every people must interpret its own history in the light of its own traditions and experience. At the same time, the history of every people must be written from without, if only to provide a necessary perspective; sooner or later the history of every people must flow from the clash of viewpoints and sensibilities.

But for historians of the South there is a more compelling reason for black and white scholars to live with each other: there is simply no way of learning about either blacks or whites without learning about the other. If it is true, as I suspect, that future generations of black scholars will bring a special viewpoint to Southern history, then their success or failure will rest, in part, on their willingness to teach us something new about the masters as well as the slaves.

I should like to consider some debilitating assumptions often brought by social historians to the study of the lower classes and to suggest a way of avoiding the twin elitist notions that these classes are generally either passive or on the brink of insurrection. We have so many books on slavery in the Old South that specialists need to devote full time merely to keeping abreast of the literature. Yet there is not one book and only a few scattered articles on life in the slave quarters: we must rely mainly on such primary and undigested sources as slave narratives and plantation memoirs. A good student might readily be able to answer questions about the economics of the plantation, the life of the planters, the politics of slavery expansionism, or a host of other matters, but he is not likely to know much about the daily life and thoughts of slaves, about the relationship of field to house slaves, or about the relationships between slave driver or foreman and other slaves. To make matters worse, he may well think he knows a good deal, for the literature abounds in undocumented assertions and plausible legends.

The fact remains that there has not been a single study of the slave driver—the most important slave on the larger plantations—and only a few sketchy and misleading studies of house slaves. So far as the life of the quarters is concerned, it should be enough to note that the idea persists, in the face of abundant evidence, that slaves had no family life to speak of. Historians and sociologists, both white and black, have been guilty of reasoning deductively from purely legal evidence—slave marriages were not recognized by law in the United States—and have done little actual research.

I do not propose here to discuss the slave family in detail, or house slaves and drivers for that matter, but should like to touch on all three in order to illustrate a larger point. We have made a grave error in the way in which we have viewed slave life, and this error has been perpetuated by both whites and blacks, racists and anti-racists. The traditional proslavery view and that of such later apologists for white supremacy as Ulrich B. Phillips have treated the blacks as objects of white benevolence and fear—as people who need both protection and control—and devoted attention to the ways in which black slaves adjusted to the demands of the master class. Abolitionist propaganda and the later and now dominant liberal viewpoint have insisted that the slave regime was so brutal and dehumanizing that blacks should be seen primarily as victims. Both these viewpoints treat black people almost wholly as objects, never as creative participants in a social process, never as half of a two-part subject.

True, abolitionists and liberal views have taken account of the ways in which slaves resisted their masters by shirking, breaking their tools, and even rebelling, but the proslavery view generally noted that much, too, even if from a different interpretation. Neither has ever stopped to consider, for example, that the evidence might reflect less a deliberate attempt at sabotage or alleged Negro inferiority than a set of attitudes toward time, work, and leisure which black people developed partly in Africa and partly in the slave quarters and which constituted a special case of a general pattern of behavior associated with preindustrial cultures.

Preindustrial peoples knew all about hard work and discipline, but their standards were neither those of the factory nor those of the plantation, and were embedded in a radically different culture. Yet even such sympathetic historians as Kenneth Stampp who give some attention to the subject of slaves generally try to show that slaves exercised some degree of autonomy in their responses to the blows or cajoling of their masters. We have yet to receive a respectful treatment—apart from some brief but suggestive passages in the work of W. E. B. Du Bois, C. L. R. James, and perhaps one or two others—of their attempts to achieve an autonomous life within the narrow limits of the slave plantation. Although family letters and plantation diaries of the whites, slave narratives, and black folklore are full of the hints and data needed for such a history, we have yet to have a synthetic record of their incessant struggle to escape from the culture as well as from the psychological domination of the master class.

In commenting briefly on certain features of family life, house slaves, and drivers, I should like to suggest some of the possibilities in an approach that goes beyond the question, What was done to the slaves? Namely: What did the slaves do for themselves and how did they do it? In a more extensive presentation it would be possible, indeed necessary, to dicuss slave religion, entertainment, songs, and dances, and many other things. But perhaps we may settle for a moment on one observation about slave religion.

We are told a great deal about the religious instruction of the slaves, by which is meant the attempt to inculcate a version of Protestant Christianity. Sometimes this instruction is interpreted as a good thing in itself and sometimes as a kind of brainwashing, but we may leave this question aside. Recently, Vincent Harding, following Du Bois's suggestive probing, has offered a different perspective and suggested that the slaves had their own way of taking up Christianity and forging it into a weapon of active resistance. Certainly we must be struck by the appearance of one or another kind of messianic preacher in almost every slave revolt on record. Professor Harding therefore asks that we look at the slaves as active participants in their own religious experience and not merely as objects being worked on by slaveholding ideologues.

This argument may be carried further to suggest that a distinctly black religion, at least in embryo, appeared in the slave quarters and played a role in shaping the daily lives of the slaves. In other words, quite apart from the problem of religion as a factor in overt resistance to slavery, we need to know how the slaves developed a religious life that enabled them to survive as autonomous human beings with a culture of their own within the white master's world.

One of the reasons we know so little about this side of slavery—and about all lower-class life—is that it is undramatic. Historians, white and black, conservative, liberal and radical, tend to look for the heroic moments, either to praise or to excoriate them. Yet, if a slave helped to keep himself psychologically intact by breaking his master's hoe, he might also have achieved the same result by a special effort to come to terms with his God, or by loving a woman who shared his burdens, or even by aspiring to be the best worker on the plantation.

We tend to think of someone who aspires to be a good slave as an Uncle Tom, and maybe we should. But human beings are not so simple. If a slave aspires to a certain excellence within the system, and if his implicit trust in the generous response of the master is betrayed, as often it must be in such a system, then he is likely to be transformed into a rebel. If so, he is likely to become the most dangerous kind of rebel, first because of his smashed illusions and second because of the skills and self-control he taught himself while he was an Uncle Tom. The historical record is full of people who were model slaves right up until the moment they killed their overseer, ran away, burned down the Big House, or joined an insurrection.

So what can be said about the decidedly non-Christian element in the religion of the slave quarters? The planters tell us repeatedly in their memoirs and letters that every plantation had its conjurer, its voodoo man, its witch doctor. To the planters this meant a residue of African superstition, and it is of course possible that by the 1830s all that remained in the slave quarters were local superstitions rather than continuing elements of the highly sophisticated religions originally brought from Africa. But the evidence suggests the emergence of an indigenous and unique combination of African and European religious ideas, adapted to the specific conditions of slave life by talented and imaginative individuals, and representing an attempt to establish a spiritual life adequate to the task of linking the slaves with the powerful culture of the masters while providing for a high degree of separation and cultural autonomy.

When we know enough of this story we shall know a good deal about the way in which the culture of an oppressed people develops. We often hear the expression "defenseless slaves," but although any individual at any given moment may be defenseless, a whole people rarely if ever is. A people may be on the defensive and dangerously exposed, but it often finds its own ways to survive and fight back. The trouble is that we keep looking for overt rebellious actions—a strike, a revolt, a murder, arson, tool-breaking—and often fail to realize that in given conditions and at particular times the wisdom of a people and their experience in struggle may dictate a different course, one of keeping together. From this point of view, the most ignorant of the field slaves who followed the conjurer of the plantation was saying no to the boss and seeking a form of cultural autonomy. That the conjurer may in any one case have been a fraud and even a kind of extortionist, and in another case a genuine popular religious leader, is, from this point of view, of little importance.

Let us take the family as an illustration. Slave law refused to recognize slave marriages and family ties. In this respect United States slavery was far worse than Spanish American or Luso-Brazilian slavery. In those Catholic cultures the Church demanded and tried to guarantee that slaves be permitted to marry and that the sanctity of the slave family be upheld. As a result, generations of American historians have concluded that American slaves had no family life and that Cuban and Brazilian slaves did.

This judgment will not bear examination. The slave trade to the United States was closed early: no later than 1808—except for some cases of smuggling which are statistically insignificant—and in fact decades earlier for most states. The rise of the Cotton Kingdom and the great period of slavery expansion followed the closing of the slave trade. Slavery, in the numbers we are accustomed to thinking of, was a product of the period following the end of African importations. The slave force that was liberated during and after the War for Southern Independence was overwhelmingly a slave force born and raised in this country.

We have good statistics on the rate of increase of that slave population and there can be no doubt that it compared roughly to that of the whites—apart from the factor of immigration—and that, furthermore, it was unique among New World plantation slave classes. An early end to the slave trade, followed by a boom in cotton and plantation slavery, dictated a policy of encouraging slave births. In contrast, the slave trade remained open to Cuba and to Brazil until the second half of the nineteenth century; as a result, there was little economic pressure to encourage family life and slave-raising. In Brazil and Cuba far more men than women were imported from Africa until late in the history of the respective slave regimes; in the Old South a rough sexual parity was established fairly early. If, therefore, religion and law militated in favor of slave families in Cuba and Brazil and against them in the Old South, economic pressure worked in reverse. The result was a self-reproducing slave force in the United States and nowhere else, so far as the statistics reveal.

It may be objected that the outcome could have reflected selective breeding rather than family stability. But selective breeding was tried in the Caribbean and elsewhere and never worked; there is no evidence that it was ever tried on a large scale in the South. Abolitionists charged that Virginia and Maryland deliberately raised slaves—not merely encouraged but actually fostered slave breeding. There is, however, no evidence for slave breeding on a significant scale. If slave-raising farms existed and if the planters were not complete fools, they would have concentrated on recruiting women of childbearing age and used a relatively small number of studs. Sample studies of major slave-exporting counties in Virginia and Maryland show no significant deviations from the patterns in Mississippi or other slave-buying regions.

It is clear that Virginia and Maryland—and other states as well—exported their natural increase for some decades before the war. But this was a process, not a policy. It reflected the economic pressures to supplement a waning income from agriculture by occasional slave sales; it was not incompatible with the encouragement of slave families and in fact reinforced it. Similarly, planters in the cotton states could not work their slaves to death and then buy fresh ones, for prices were too high. They had been too high from the very moment the Cotton Kingdom began its westward march and, therefore, a tradition of slave-killing never did take root. As time went on, the pressures mounted to provide slaves with enough material and even psychological satisfaction to guarantee the minimum morale needed for reproduction.

These standards of treatment—food, living space, time off, etc.—became part of the prevailing standard of decency, not easily violated by greedy slaveholders. In some respects the American slave system may have been the worst in the world, as Elkins and others insist. But in purely material terms, it was probably the best, for the evidence left by participants, travelers, and official reports shows that American slaves were generally better fed, clothed, housed, and worked than those of Cuba, Jamaica, Brazil, or elsewhere.

But the important thing here is that the prevailing standard of decency was not easily violated because the slaves had come to understand their own position. If a master wished to keep his plantation going, he had to learn the limits of his slaves' endurance.

If, for example, he decided to ignore the prevailing custom of giving Sundays off or of giving an extended Christmas holiday, his slaves would feel sorely tried and would certainly pay him back with one or another form of destruction. The slaves remained in a weak position, but they were rarely completely helpless, and by guile, brute courage, and a variety of other devices they taught every master just where the line was he dared not cross if he wanted a crop. In precisely this way, slaves took up the masters' interest in their family life and turned it to account. The typical plantation in the Upper South and the Lower was organized by family units. Man and wife lived together with children, and to a considerable degree the man was in fact the man in the house.

Whites violated black family life in several ways. Many families were disrupted by slave sales, especially in the Upper South where economic pressures were strong; white men on the plantations could and often did violate black women: nothing can minimize these injustices. The frequency of sales is extremely hard to measure. Many slaves were troublesome and sold many times over; this inflated the total number of sales but obscured the incidence of individual transfers.

The crimes against black people are a matter of record, and no qualifications can soften their impact. But it is not at all certain that most slaves did not live stable married lives in the quarters despite the pressures of the market. I do not wish to take up the vexing question of the violation of black women here, but certainly there was enough of it to justify the anger of those who condemned the regime on this ground alone. The evidence, however, does not warrant an assumption that a large percentage of black plantation women were so violated. In other words, for a judgment on the moral quality of the regime, the problem was extremely important; for an assessment of the normal life of the slaves it was much less so.

What the sources show—both the plantation diaries and record books and letters of the masters and also the reports of runaway slaves and ex-slaves—is that the average plantation slave lived in a family setting, developed strong family ties, and held the nuclear family as the proper social norm. It is true that planters who often had to excuse others, or even themselves, for breaking up families by sale, would sometimes argue that blacks did not really form deep and lasting attachments, that they lacked a strong family sense, that they were naturally promiscuous, and so forth. Abolitionists and former slaves would reinforce the prevalent notion by saying that slavery was so horrible no real family tie could be maintained. Since planters, abolitionists, and former slaves all said the same thing, it has usually been taken as the truth. Only it was not.

In the first place, these various sources also say the opposite, which we rarely notice. Planters agonized over the breakup of families and repeatedly expressed regrets and dismay. Often, they went to great lengths to keep families together at considerable expense, for they knew how painful it was to enforce separations. Whether they were motivated by such material considerations as maintaining plantation morale or by more lofty sentiments is beside the point. They often demonstrated that they knew very well how strong the family ties were in the quarters. Planters encouraged the slaves to live together in stable units, for they recognized that a man was easier to control if he had a wife and children to worry about.

The slaves, on their side, behaved, of course, in various ways. Some were indeed promiscuous, although much of the charge of promiscuity stemmed not so much from actual promiscuity as from sequential polygamy. They did change partners more often than Victorian whites said they could stomach. (In this respect, they might be considered among the forerunners of the white middle-class sexual morality of the 1960s.) I stress these matters, the interest of the master in slave family stability and the effort of the slave to protect his stake in a home, however impoverished, because it is now fashionable to believe that black people came out of slavery with little or no sense of family life. But if so, then we need to know why so many thousands wandered over the South during early Reconstruction looking for their spouses or children.

We do not know just how many slaves lived as a family or were willing and able to maintain a stable family life during slavery. But the number was certainly great, whatever the percentage, and as a result, the social norm that black people carried from slavery to freedom was that of the nuclear family. If it is true that the black family has disintegrated in the ghettos—and we have yet to see conclusive evidence of this—then the source will have to be found in the conditions of economic and social oppression imposed upon blacks during recent decades. The experience of slaves, for all its tragic disruptions, pointed toward a stable postslavery family life, and recent scholarship demonstrates conclusively that the reconstruction and postreconstruction black experience carried forward the acceptance of the nuclear-family norm.

Let us consider the role of the male and the legend of a slave matriarchy. Almost all writers on slavery describe the slave man as a guest in the house, who could have no role beyond a purely sexual one. The slave narratives and the diaries and letters of white plantation owners tell us something else. The position of the male slave was undeniably precarious and frustrating. If his wife was to be whipped, he had to stand by and watch; he could not fully control his own children; he was not a breadwinner in the usual sense. There were severe restrictions imposed upon the manifestations of what we somewhat erroneously call manliness. But both masters and former slaves tell us about some plantations on which certain women were not easily or often punished because it was readily understood that to punish the woman it would be necessary to kill her man first.

These cases were the exception, but they tell us that the man felt a duty to protect his woman. If circumstances conspired to prevent his fulfilling that duty, those circumstances often included the fact that his woman did not expect him to do so and indeed consoled him by acknowledging the futility of such a gesture. We cannot know what was said between a man and a woman when they lay down together at night after having experienced such outrages, but there are enough hints in the slave narratives to suggest that both knew what a man could do, as well as what he "should" do, especially when there were children to consider. Many scholars suggested that black women treated their men with contempt for not doing what circumstances made impossible. This is a deduction from tenuous assumptions; it is not a demonstrated fact.

Beyond that, the man of the house did do various things. He trapped and hunted animals to supplement the diet in the quarters, and in this small but important and symbolic way he was a breadwinner. He organized the garden plot and presided over the division of labor with his wife. He disciplined his children—or divided that function with his wife as people in other circumstances do—and generally was the source of authority in the cabin. This relationship within the family was not alway idyllic. In many instances, he imposed his authority over both wife and children by force. Masters forbade men to hit their wives and children and whipped them for it; but they did it anyway and often. And there is not much evidence that women readily ran to the masters to ask that their husbands be whipped for striking them.

The evidence on these matters, even from the slave narratives, is fragmentary, but what it suggests is that the men asserted their authority as best they could; that the women expected to have to defer to their husbands in certain matters; and that both tried hard to keep the master out of their lives. The conditions were unfavorable, and perhaps many men did succumb and in one way or another became emasculated. But we might also reflect on the ways in which black men and women conspired to maintain their own sense of dignity and their own autonomy by settling things among themselves and thereby asserting their own personalities.

Black women have often been praised—and justly so—for their strength and determination in holding their families together during slavery, when the man was supposedly put aside or rendered irrelevant. It is time, I think, to praise them for another thing which large numbers of them seem to have been able to do: to support a man they loved in ways deep enough and varied enough to help him to resist the mighty forces for dehumanization and emasculation. Without the support of their women, not many black men could have survived; but with it—and there is plenty of testimony that they often had it—many could and did.

If our failure to see the plantation from the vantage point of the slave quarters has led us to substitute abstractions for research on the slave family, so has it saddled us with unsubstantiated and erroneous ideas on house slaves. According to the legend, house slaves were the Uncle Toms of the system—a privileged caste apart, contemptuous of the field hands, jealous of their place in the affection or at least attention of the white master and mistress, and generally sellouts, "white man's niggers." Like most stereotypes this one has its kernel of truth; there were indeed many house slaves who fit the description. But in 1860 roughly half the slaves in the South lived on farms of twenty or fewer slaves; another 25 percent lived on plantations of between twenty and fifty slaves. Only 25 percent, in other words, lived on plantations of fifty or more, and of these, the majority lived on units of fewer than 100—that is, on units of fewer than twenty slave families. In short, the typical house slave worked either on a small farm or, at best, on a moderate-sized plantation. Only a few lived and worked on plantations large enough to permit the formation of a separate group of house slaves—of enough house slaves to form a caste unto themselves.

The idea of the fancy-dressed, uppity, self-inflated house slave who despised the field blacks and identified with the whites derives from those who lived in the towns and cities like Charleston, New Orleans, Natchez, and Richmond. These town house slaves and a small group of privileged house slaves on huge plantations could and sometimes did form a separate caste having the qualities attributed to them in the literature. Certainly the big planters and their families, who left most of the white family records that have been the major source, would likely have remembered precisely these slaves. Even these blacks deserve a more careful look than they have received, for they were much more complicated people than we have been led to believe. The important point, however, is that the typical house slave was far removed from this condition. He, or more likely she, worked with perhaps one to three or four others on an estate too small to permit any such caste formation.

If the typical house slave was an Uncle Tom and a spoiled child of the whites, then we need to be told just why so many of them turn up in the records of runaways. There is abundant evidence from the war years. We hear much about the faithful retainers who held the Yankees off from the Big House, or protected young missus, or hid the family silver. Such types were not at all rare. But they do not appear to have been nearly so numerous as those house slaves who joined the field slaves in fleeing to the Yankee lines when the opportunity arose.

The best sources on this point are the letters and diaries of the planters themselves who were shocked at the defection of their favorite slaves. From a vast body of published and unpublished writing by Southern whites on their war experience we learn that they could readily understand the defection of the field hands, whom they considered stupid and easily led, but were unable to account for the flight—with expressions sometimes of regret and sometimes of anger and hatred—of their house slaves. They had always thought that they knew these blacks, loved them, were loved by them; and they considered them part of the family. One day they learned that they had been deceiving themselves, that they had been living intimately with people they did not know at all. The house slaves, when the opportunity presented itself, responded with the same range of behavior as did the field slaves: they proved themselves to be just as often rebellious and independent as docile and loyal.

This display of independence really was nothing new. If it is true that house slaves were often regarded as traitors to the black cause during slave rebellions, it is also true that their appearance in those rebellions was not so rare as we are led to believe. Consider the evidence from the abortive slave rebellion led by Denmark Vesey in Charleston in 1822. One slave leader, in an often-quoted remark, said not to trust the house slaves because they were too closely tied to the whites, and, indeed, several house slaves did turn informers. But we ought also to note that some of the toughest and most devoted leaders of Vesey's rebellion were themselves house slaves. Indeed, the greatest scandal was the role played by the most trusted slaves of the governor of South Carolina.

Certainly, the role of the house slave was always ambiguous and often treacherous. But if many house slaves betrayed their fellows, many others collected information in the Big House and passed it on to the quarters. We know how well informed the field slaves were about movements of Yankee troops during the war; we know that these field slaves fled to the Yankee lines with uncanny accuracy in timing and direction. Probably no group was more influential in providing the necessary information than those same house slaves who are so often denigrated.

The decision of slaves, whether house slaves or not, to protect whites during slave insurrections or other catastrophes, hardly proves them to have been Toms. The master-slave relationship, especially when it occurred in the intimacies of the Big House, was always profoundly ambivalent. Many of the same slaves who protected their masters and mistresses from harm and thereby asserted their own humanity were anything but docile creatures of the whites.

Since most house slaves worked on estates too small for a separate existence, their social life was normally down in the slave quarters and not apart or with the whites. Women usually predominated in the house, and even when they did not, the group was too small for natural pairing off. A large number of house slaves married field hands, or more likely the more skilled artisans or workers. Under such circumstances, the line between house slaves and field hands was not sharp for most slaves. Except on the really large plantations, house slaves were expected to help out in the fields during picking season and during emergencies. The average house slave got a periodic taste of field work and had little opportunity to cultivate airs.

There are two general features to the question of house slaves that deserve comment: first, there is the ambiguity of their situation and its resultant ambivalence toward whites; the other is the significance of the house slave in the formation of a distinctly Afro-American culture. The one point I should insist upon in any analysis of the house slave is ambivalence. It is impossible to think of people, black and white, slave and master, thrown together in the intimacy of the Big House without realizing that they had to emerge loving and hating each other.

Life together meant sharing pains and problems, confiding secrets, having company when no one else would do, being forced to help one another in a multitude of ways. It also meant experiencing in common, but in tragically opposite ways, the full force of lordship and bondage: that is, the full force of petty tyranny imposed by one woman on another; of expecting someone to be at one's beck and call regardless of her own feelings and wishes; of being able to take out one's frustrations and disappointments on an innocent bystander, who would no doubt be guilty enough of something since servants are always falling short of expectations.

To illustrate the complexity of black slave behavior in the Big House, let us take a single illustration. It is typical in that it catches the ambiguity of those enmeshed and yet hostile lives. Beyond that it is of course unique, as is all individual experience. Eliza L. Magruder was the niece of a deceased planter and politician from the Natchez, Mississippi, region and went to live with her aunt Olivia, who managed the old plantation herself. Eliza kept a diary for the years 1846 and 1847 and then again for 1854 to 1857. She may have kept a diary for the intermittent years, but none has been found. In any case, she has a number of references to a slave woman, Annica, and a few to another, Lavinia. We have here four women, two white and two black, two mistresses and two servants, thrown together in a single house and forced on one another's company all year long, year after year.

On August 17, 1846, Eliza wrote in her diary more or less in passing, "Aunt Olivia whipped Annica for obstinacy." This chastisement had followed incidents in which Annica had been "impudent." About a month later, on September 11, Annica took another whipping—for "obstinacy." Eliza appears to have been a bit squeamish, for her tone, if we read it correctly, suggests that she was not accustomed to witnessing such unpleasantness. On January 24, 1847, she confided to her diary, "I feel badly. Got very angry and whipped Lavinia. O! for government over my temper." But as the world progresses, so did Eliza's fortitude in the fact of others' adversity. When her diary resumed in 1854, she had changed slightly: the squeamishness had diminished. Annica had not changed: she remained her old, saucy self. October 26, 1854: "Boxed Annica's ears for impertinence."

Punctuated by this war of wills, daily life went on. Annica's mother lived in Jackson, Mississippi, and mother and daughter kept in touch. Since Annica could neither read nor write, Eliza served as her helpmate and confidante. December 5, 1854: "I wrote for Annica to her mother." Annica's mother wrote back in due time, no doubt to Annica's satisfaction, but also to her discomfiture. As Eliza observed on January 25, 1855, "Annica got a letter from her mammy which detected her in a lie. O! that negroes generally were more truthful." So we ought not to be sur-

prised that Eliza could write without a trace of the old squeamishness on July 11, 1855, "I whipt Annica."

The impertinent Annica remained undaunted. November 29,
1855: "Aunt Olivia gave Annica a good scolding and made her ask
my pardon and will punish her otherwise." Perhaps we should con-
clude that Annica's behavior had earned the undying enmity of
the austere white ladies, but some doubts may be permitted. On
July 24, 1856, several of their neighbors set out on a trip to Jackson, Mississippi, where, it will be recalled, Annica's mother lived.
Aunt Olivia, with Eliza's concurrence, sent Annica along for a two-
week holiday and provided ten dollars for her expenses. On August
3, Annica returned home in time for breakfast.

On September 4, 1856, "Annica was very impertinent, and
I boxed her ears." Three days later, wrote Eliza, "I kept Annica in
in the afternoon for impudence." The next day (September 8)
Eliza told Aunt Olivia about Annica's misconduct. "She reproved
her for it and will I suppose punish her in some way." Again in
November, on the tenth day of the month, "Aunt Olivia whipt
Annica for impertinence."

At this point, after a decade of impudence, impertinence,
obstinacy, whipping, and ear-boxing, one might expect that Annica
would have been dispatched to the cotton fields. But she remained
in the Big House. And what shall we make of such an incident as
occurred on the night of December 29, 1856, when poor Annica
was ill and in great pain? It is not so much that Eliza sat up with
her, doing what she could; it is rather that she seemed both concerned and conscious of performing a simple duty. On the assumption that the illness left Annica weak for a while, Eliza of course
still had Lavinia. January 30, 1857: "I boxed Lavinia's ears for
coming up late when I told her not."

On April 23, 1857, Annica greatly pleased Eliza by making
her a white bonnet. But by April 26, Annica was once again making trouble: "Aunt Olivia punished Annica by keeping her in her
room all afternoon." And the next day: "Aunt Olivia had Annica
locked up in the garret all day. I pray it may humble her and make
further punishment unnecessary."

On August 18, 1857, "Aunt Olivia held a court of enquiry,
but didn't find out who ripped my pattern." There is no proof
that Annica did it; still, one wonders. Two weeks later in Miss
Eliza's Sunday school, "Annica was strongly tempted to misbe-
have. I brought her in however." The entries end here.

Let us suppose that the ladies had carried their household
into the war years: What then? It would take little imagination to

see Annica's face and to hear her tone as she marched into the kitchen to announce her departure for the federal lines. It would not even take much imagination to see her burning the house down. Yet she seems never to have been violent, and we should not be too quick to assume that she would easily have left the only home that she had known as an adult and the women who wrote letters to her mother, exchanged confidences with her, and stayed up with her on feverish nights. The only thing we can be sure of is that she remained impudent to the day she died.

What I think this anecdote demonstrates above all is the ambivalence of relations in the Big House and the stubborn struggle for individuality that house slaves, with or without the whip, were capable of. Yet it may also hint at another side of their experience and thereby help to explain why so many black militants, like so many historians before them, are quick to condemn the whole house-slave legacy as one to be exorcized. The house slaves were indeed close to the whites, and of all the black groups they exhibit the most direct adherence to certain white cultural standards. In their religious practices, their dress, their manners, their prejudices, they were undoubtedly the black group most influenced by Euro-American culture. But this kind of cultural accommodationism was by no means the same thing as docility or Uncle Tomism. Even a relatively assimilated house slave could and normally did strike back, assert independence, and resist arbitrariness and oppression.

We are today accustomed to thinking of black nationalists as "militants" and civil rights integrationists as "moderates," "conservatives," or something worse. Yet Dr. Martin Luther King and his followers were and are militant integrationists, prepared to give up their lives for their people; on the other hand, there are plenty of black nationalists who are anything but militant. The tension between integration and separatism has always rent the black community, but now it has led us to confuse questions of militancy with those of nationalism. In fact, the combinations vary; there is no convincing way to categorize integrationists or separationists as either militant or accommodating. Field hands or house slaves could be either docile, "accommodating," or rebellious, and it is likely that most were all at once.

If today the house slaves have a bad press, it is largely because of their cultural assimilationism, from which it is erroneously deduced that they were docile. The first point may be well taken; the second is not. LeRoi Jones, for example, in his book *Blues People*, argues convincingly that field slaves had forged the rudiments of a distinct Afro-American culture, whereas the house slaves largely took over the culture of the whites. He writes primarily about black music, but he might easily extend his analysis to language and other fields. There are clearly two ways of looking at this side of the house-slave experience. On the one hand, the house slaves reinforced white culture in the slave quarters; they were one of the Americanizing elements in the black community; on the other hand, they wittingly or unwittingly served as agents of white repression of an indigenous Afro-American national culture.

Of course, both these statements are really the same; it is merely that they differ in their implicit judgments. But we ought to remember that this role did not reduce the house slaves who were in their own way often rebellious and independent in their behavior. Therefore, even these slaves, notwithstanding their assimilationist outlook and action, also contributed in no small degree to the tradition of survival and resistance to oppression that today inspires the black liberation movement.

If today we are inclined to accept uncritically the contemptuous attitude that some critics have toward the house slave, we might ponder the reflections of the great black pianist Cecil Taylor. Taylor was speaking in the mid-1960s—a century after slavery—but he was speaking of his father in a way that I think applies to what might be said of house slaves. Taylor was talking to A. B. Spellman, as reported in Spellman's book, *Four Lives in the Bebop Business:*

> Music to me was in a way holding on to Negro culture, because there wasn't much of it around. My father has a great store of knowledge about black folklore. He could talk about how it was with the slaves in the 1860's, about the field shouts and hollers, about myths of black people. . . . He worked out in Long Island for a State Senator. He was a house servant and a chef at the Senator's sanatorium for wealthy mental wrecks. And actually it was my father more than the Senator himself who raised the Senator's children. . . .
>
> And I really used to get dragged at my father for taking such shit off these people. I didn't dig his being a house servant. I really didn't understand my old man; well, you're my generation and you know the difference between us and our fathers. Like, they had to be strong men to take what they took. But of course we didn't see it that way. So that I feel now that I really didn't understand my father, who was a really lovely cat. He used to tell me to stay cool, not to get excited. He had a way of letting other people display their emotions while keeping control of his own. People used to say to me, "Cecil, you'll never be the gentleman your father was." That's true. My father was quite a gentleman. . . . I wish that I had taken down more about all that he knew about black folklore, because that's lost too; he died in 1961.

Finally, we must consider another misunderstood group of slaves—the drivers. These black slave foremen were chosen by the master to work under his direction or that of an overseer and to keep the hands moving. They would rouse the field slaves in the morning and check their cabins at night; would take responsibility for their performance; and often would be the ones to lay the whip across their backs. In the existing literature the drivers appear as ogres, monsters, betrayers, and sadists. Sometimes they were. Yet Mrs. Willie Lee Rose, in her book *Rehearsal for Reconstruction*, notes that it was the drivers in the Sea Islands who kept the plantations together after the masters had fled the approach of the Yankees, who kept up discipline, and who led the blacks during those difficult days.

Now, it is obvious that if the drivers were as they are reported to have been, they would have had their throats cut as soon as their white protectors had left. In my own researches for the war years I have found repeatedly, almost monotonously, that when the slaves fled the plantations or else took over plantations deserted by the whites, the drivers emerged as the leaders. Moreover, the runaway records from the North and from Canada reveal that a number of drivers were among those who successfully escaped the South.

One clue to the actual state of affairs may be found in the agricultural journals for which many planters and overseers wrote about plantation matters. Overseers often complained bitterly that masters trusted their drivers more than they trusted them. They charged that often overseers would be fired at the driver's instigation and that, in general, masters were too close to their drivers and too hostile and suspicious toward their white overseers. The planters did not deny the charges; rather, they admitted them and defended themselves by arguing that the drivers were slaves who had earned their trust and that they had to have some kind of check on their overseers. Overseers were changed every two or three years on most plantations whereas drivers remained in their jobs endlessly. Usually any given driver remained in his position while a parade of overseers came and went.

It had to be so. The slaves had to be controlled if production was to be on schedule, but only romantics would think that a whip could effect the result. The actual amount of work done and the quality of life on the plantation were a consequence of a compromise between masters and slaves. It was a grossly unfair and one-sided compromise, with the master holding a big edge. But the slaves did not simply lie down and take whatever came.

They had their own ways of foot-dragging, dissembling, delaying, and sabotaging.

The role of the driver was to minimize the friction by mediating between the Big House and the quarters. On the one hand he was the master's man: he obeyed orders, inflicted punishments, and stood for authority and discipline. On the other hand, he could and did tell the master that the overseer was too harsh, too irregular; that he was incapable of holding the respect of the hands; that he was a bungler. The slaves generally knew just how much they had to put up with under a barbarous labor system but they also knew what even that system regarded as going too far. The driver was their voice in the Big House as he was the master's voice in the quarters.

Former slaves tell us of drivers who were sadistic monsters, but they also tell us of drivers who did everything possible to soften punishments and to protect the slaves as best they could. It was an impossible situation, but there is little evidence that drivers were generally hated by the field hands.

The selection of a driver was a difficult matter for a master. First, the driver had to be a strong man, capable of bullying rather than of being bullied. Second, he had to be uncommonly intelligent and capable of understanding a good deal about plantation management. A driver had to command respect in the quarters. It would be possible to get along for a while with a brutal driver who could rule by fear, but, generally, planters understood that respect and acquiescence were as important as fear and that a driver had to do more than make others afraid of him. It was then necessary to pick a man who had leadership qualities in the eyes of the slaves.

The drivers commanded respect in various ways. Sometimes they became preachers among the slaves and got added prestige that way. Sometimes, possibly quite often, they acted as judge and jury in the quarters. Disputes among slaves arose often, generally about women and family matters. If there were fights or bitter quarrels and if they were called to the attention of the overseer or the master, the end would be a whipping for one or more participants. Under such circumstances, the driver was the natural choice of the slaves themselves to arbitrate knotty problems. With such roles in and out of the quarters, it is no wonder that so many drivers remained leaders during and after the war, when the blacks had the choice of discarding them and following others.

Every kind of plantation had two kinds of so-called "bad niggers." The first kind were those so designated by the masters because they were recalcitrant. The second kind were those so designated by the slaves themselves. These were slaves who may or may not have troubled the master directly but were a problem to their fellow slaves because they stole, or bullied, or abused other men's women. The driver was in a position to know what was happening in the quarters and to intervene to protect weaker or more timid slaves against these bullies. In short, the driver's position was highly ambiguous and on balance was probably more often than not positive from the slaves' point of view. Whatever the intentions of the master, even in the selection of his own foremen—his own men, as it were—the slaves generally were not passive, not objects, but active agents who helped to shape events, even if within narrow limits and with great difficulty.

We know that there were not many slave revolts in the South and that those that did occur were small and local. There were good reasons for the low incidence of rebellion: In general, the balance of forces was such that revolt meant suicide. Under such conditions, black slaves struggled to live as much as possible on their own terms. If their actions were less bombastic and heroic than romantic historians would like us to believe, they were nonetheless impressive in their assertion of their resourcefulness and dignity, and a strong sense of self and community. Had they not been, the fate of black America after emancipation would have been even grimmer than it was. For the most part the best that the slaves could do was to live, not merely physically but with as much inner autonomy as was humanly possible.

Every man has his own judgment of heroism, but the kind of heroism alluded to by Cecil Taylor in his moving tribute to his father is worth recalling. There are moments in the history of every people—and sometimes these historical moments are centuries—in which they cannot do more than succeed in keeping themselves together and maintaining a sense of individual dignity and collective identity. Slavery was such a moment for black people in America, and their performance during it bequeathed a legacy that combined negative elements to be exorcized with the decisive elements of community and self-discipline. If one were to tax even the privileged house slaves or drivers with the question, "Where were you when your people were groaning under the lash," they could, if they chose, answer with a paraphrase of the Abbé Sieyès, but proudly and without his cynicism, "We were with our people, and together we survived."

Slave Songs
and
Slave Consciousness

LAWRENCE W. LEVINE

Lawrence Levine believes that written records cannot convey the full compass or meaning of slave life. As a preliterate people, Afro-American slaves expressed their values and hopes through music, oral tradition, and religious practice. In his convincing book, *Black Culture and Black Consciousness: Afro-American Folk Thought from Slavery to Freedom* (1977), Levine demonstrated that imaginative use of such non-literary sources can unveil much about the evolution of slave culture and social structure. In this essay he explores folksongs and spirituals in order to enter slave culture and to come to know the slaves on their own terms. He discovers a dynamic religion infusing slave life and giving slaves an identity as a separate and worthy people. In their sacred songs the slaves revealed artistry and strong, although not complete, African ties in the manner that they ordered time and nature. In what ways did the spirituals reflect the ethos of the slave community? What was the eschatology of the slaves' religion? How did this eschatology influence the slaves' self-perceptions and actions in this world? How did the slaves' conceptions of time and nature affect their lives as slaves? Does the content of the slaves' sacred songs suggest that the masters, who enjoyed the slaves' singing and often

From Lawrence W. Levine, "Slave Songs and Slave Consciousness: An Exploration in Neglected Sources," in *Anonymous Americans*, Tamara K. Hareven, ed., © 1971, pp. 114-126. Reprinted by permission of Prentice-Hall, Inc., Englewood Cliffs, New Jersey.

boasted about it, did not really understand their slaves, much less control them? Compare Levine's conclusions about the social thrust of slave religion with Genovese's arguments. Compare his suggestions about the redefinition of African culture in the slave community with the arguments of Wood and Mullin in the first two selections and the arguments of Charles Joyner in the final reading.

It is significant that the most common form of slave music we know of is sacred song. I use the term "sacred" not in its present usage as something antithetical to the secular world; neither the slaves nor their African forebears ever drew modernity's clear line between the sacred and the secular. The uses to which spirituals were put are an unmistakable indication of this. They were not sung solely or even primarily in churches or praise houses, but were used as rowing songs, field songs, work songs, and social songs. On the Sea Islands during the Civil War, Lucy McKim heard the spiritual "Poor Rosy" sung in a wide variety of contexts and tempos.

> On the water, the oars dip "Poor Rosy" to an even andante; a stout boy and girl at the hominy-mill will make the same "Poor Rosy" fly, to keep up with the whirling stone; and in the evening, after the day's work is done, "Heab'n shall-a be my home" [the final line of each stanza] peals up slowly and mournfully from the distant quarters.[1]

For the slaves, then, songs of God and the mythic heroes of their religion were not confined to any specific time or place, but were appropriate to almost every situation. It is in this sense that I use the concept sacred—not to signify a rejection of the present world but to describe the process of incorporating within this world all the elements of the divine. The religious historian Mircea Eliade, whose definition of sacred has shaped my own, has maintained that for men in traditional societies religion is a means of extending the world spatially upward so that communication with the other world becomes ritually possible, and extending it temporally backward so that the paradigmatic acts of the gods and mythical ancestors can be continually reenacted and indefinitely recoverable. By creating sacred time and space, man can perpetually live in the presence of his gods, can hold on to the certainty that within one's own lifetime "rebirth" is continually possible, and can impose order on the chaos of the universe. "Life," as Eliade puts it, "is lived on a twofold plane; it takes its course as human existence and, at the same time, shares in a transhuman life, that of the cosmos or the gods."[2]

This notion of sacredness gets at the essence of the spirituals, and through them at the essence of the slave's world view. Denied the possibility of achieving an adjustment to the external world of the antebellum South which involved meaningful forms of personal integration, attainment of status, and feelings of individual worth that all human beings crave and need, the slaves created a new world by transcending the narrow confines of the one in which they were forced to live. They extended the boundaries of their restrictive universe backward until it fused with the world of the Old Testament, and upward until it became one with the world beyond. The spirituals are the record of a people who found the status, the harmony, the values, the order they needed to survive by internally creating an expanded universe, by literally willing themselves reborn. In this respect I agree with the anthropologist Paul Radin that

> The ante-bellum Negro was not converted to God. He converted God to himself. In the Christian God he found a fixed point and he needed a fixed point, for both within and outside of himself, he could see only vacillation and endless shifting.... There was no other safety for people faced on all sides by doubt and the threat of personal disintegration, by the thwarting of instincts and the annihilation of values.[3]

The confinement of much of the slave's new world to dreams and fantasies does not free us from the historical obligation of examining its contours, weighing its implications for the development of the slave's psychic and emotional structure, and eschewing the kind of facile reasoning that leads Professor Elkins to imply that, since the slaves had no alternatives open to them, their fantasy life was "limited to catfish and watermelons."[4] Their spirituals indicate clearly that there *were* alternatives open to them—alternatives which they themselves fashioned out of the fusion of their African heritage and their new religion—and that their fantasy life was so rich and so important to them that it demands understanding if we are even to begin to comprehend their inner world.

The God the slaves sang of was neither remote nor abstract, but as intimate, personal, and immediate as the gods of Africa had

been. "O when I talk I talk wid God," "Mass Jesus is my bosom
friend," "I'm goin' to walk with [talk with, live with, see] King
Jesus by myself, by myself," were refrains that echoed through
the spirituals.[5]

> *In de mornin' when I rise,*
> *Tell my Jesus huddy [howdy] oh,*
> *I wash my hands in de mornin' glory,*
> *Tell my Jesus huddy oh.*[6]

> *Gwine to argue wid de Father and chatter wid de son,*
> *The last trumpet shall sound, I'll be there.*
> *Gwine talk 'bout de bright world dey des' come from.*
> *The last trumpet shall sound, I'll be there.*[7]

> *Gwine to write to Massa Jesus,*
> *To send some Valiant soldier*
> *To turn back Pharaoh's army, Hallelu!*[8]

The heroes of the Scriptures—"Sister Mary," "Brudder
Jonah," "Brudder Moses," "Brudder Daniel"—were greeted with
similar intimacy and immediacy. In the world of the spirituals, it
was not the masters and mistresses, but God and Jesus and the entire pantheon of Old Testament figures who set the standards, established the precedents, and defined the values: who, in short,
constituted the "significant others." The world described by the
slave songs was a black world in which no reference was ever made
to any white contemporaries. The slave's positive reference group
was composed entirely of his own peers: his mother, father, sister,
brother, uncles, aunts, preacher, fellow "sinners" and "mourners"
of whom he sang endlessely, to whom he sent messages via the
dying, and with whom he was reunited joyfully in the next world.

The same sense of sacred time and space which shaped the
slave's portraits of his gods and heroes also made his visions of the
past and future immediate and compelling. Descriptions of the
Crucifixion communicate a sense of the actual presence of the
singers: "Dey pierced Him in the side ... Dey nail Him to de
cross ... Dey rivet His feet ... Dey hanged him high ... Dey
stretch Him wide...."

> *Oh sometimes it causes me to tremble,—tremble,—tremble,*
> *Were you there when they crucified my Lord?*[9]

The Slave's "shout"—that counterclockwise, shuffling dance

which frequently occurred after the religious service and lasted long into the night—often became a medium through which the ecstatic dancers were transformed into actual participants in historic actions: Joshua's army marching around the walls of Jericho, the children of Israel following Moses out of Egypt.[10]

The thin line between time dimensions is nowhere better illustrated than in the slave's visions of the future, which were, of course, a direct negation of his present. Among the most striking spirituals are those which pile detail upon detail in describing the Day of Judgment: "You'll see de world on fire . . . see de element a meltin', . . . see the stars a fallin' . . . see the moon a bleedin'. . . see the forked lightning. . . . Hear the rumblin' thunder . . . see the righteous marching, . . . see my Jesus coming . . ," and the world to come where "Dere's no sun to burn you . . . no hard trials . . . no whips a crackin' . . . no stormy weather . . . no tribulation. . . no evil-doers . . . All is gladness in de Kingdom."[11] This vividness was matched by the slave's certainty that he would partake of the triumph of judgment and the joys of the new world:

> *Dere's room enough, room enough, room enough in de heaven,*
> *   my Lord*
> *Room enough, room enough, I can't stay behind.*[12]

Continually, the slaves sang of reaching out beyond the world that confined them, of seeing Jesus "in de wilderness," of praying "in de lonesome valley," of breathing in the freedom of the mountain peaks:

> *Did yo' ever*
> *Stan' on mountun,*
> *Wash yo' han's*
> *In a cloud?*[13]

Continually, they held out the possibility of imminent rebirth; "I look at de worl' an' de worl' look new, . . . I look at my hands an' they look so too . . . I looked at my feet, my feet was too."[14]

These possibilites, these certainties were not surprising. The religious revivals which swept large numbers of slaves into the Christian fold in the late eighteenth and early nineteenth centuries were based upon a *practical* (not necessarily theological) Armianism: God would save all who believed in Him; Salvation was there for all to take hold of if they would. The effects of this message upon the slaves who were exposed to and converted by it have been passed over too easily by historians. Those effects are illustrated graphically in the spirituals which were the products of these revivals and which continued to spread evangelical word long after the revivals had passed into history.

The religious music of the slaves is almost devoid of feelings of depravity or unworthiness, but is rather, as I have tried to show, pervaded by a sense of change, transcendence, ultimate justice, and personal worth. The spirituals have been referred to as "sorrow songs," and in some respects they were. The slaves sang of "rollin' thro' an unfriendly world," of being "a-trouble in de mind," of living in a world which was a "howling wilderness," "a hell to me," of feeling like a "motherless child," "a po' little orphan chile in de worl'," a "home-e-less child," of fearing that "Trouble will bury me down." [15]

But these feelings were rarely pervasive or permanent; almost always they were overshadowed by a triumphant note of affirmation. Even so despairing a wail as "Nobody Knows the Trouble I've Had" could suddenly have its mood transformed by lines like: "One morning I was a-walking down, . . . Saw some berries a-hanging down, . . . I pick de berry and I suck de juice, . . . Just as sweet as de honey in de comb."[16] Similarly, amid the deep sorrow of "Sometimes I feel like a Motherless chile," sudden release could come with the lines: "Sometimes I feel like/A eagle in de air. . . . Spread my wings an'/Fly, fly, fly."[17] Slaves spent little time singing of the horrors of hell or damnation. Their songs of the Devil, quoted earlier, pictured a harsh but almost semicomic figure (often, one suspects, a surrogate for the white man), over whom they triumphed with reassuring regularity. For all their inevitable sadness, slave songs were characterized more by a feeling of confidence than of despair. There was confidence that contemporary power relationships were not immutable: "Did not old Pharaoh get lost, get lost, get lost, . . . get lost in the Red Sea?"; confidence in the possibilites of instantaneous change: "Jesus make de dumb to speak. . . . Jesus make de cripple walk. . . . Jesus give de blind his sight. . . . Jesus do most anything"; confidence in the rewards of persistence: "Keep a' inching along like a poor inch-worm,/ Jesus will come by'nd bye"; confidence that nothing could stand in the way of the justice they would receive: "You kin hender me here, but you can't do it dah," "O no man, no man, can hinder me"; confidence in the prospects of the future: "We'll walk de golden streets/Of de New Jerusalem." Religion, the slaves sang, "is good for anything, . . . Religion make you happy, . . . Religion gib me patience . . . O member, get Religion . . . Religion is so sweet."[18]

The slaves often pursued the "sweetness" of their religion in the face of many obstacles. Becky Ilsey, who was 16 when she was emancipated, recalled many years later:

> 'Fo' de war when we'd have a meetin' at night, wuz mos' always 'way in de woods or de bushes some whar so de white folks couldn't hear, an' when de'd sing a spiritual an' de spirit 'gin to shout some de elders would go 'mongst de folks an' put dey han' over dey mouf an' some times put a clof in dey mouf an' say: "Spirity don talk so loud or de patterol break us up." You know dey had white patterols what went 'roun' at night to see de niggers didn't cut up no devilment, an' den de meetin' would break up an' some would go to one house an' some to er nudder an' dey woud groan er w'ile, den go home.[19]

Elizabeth Ross Hite testified that although she and her fellow slaves on a Louisiana plantation were Catholics, "lots didn't like that 'ligion."

> We used to hide between some bricks and hold church ourselves. You see, the Catholic preachers from France wouldn't let us shout, and the Lawd done said you gotta shout if you want to be saved. That's in the Bible.
>   Sometimes we held church all night long, 'til way in the mornin'. We burned some grease in a can for the preacher to see the Bible by....
>   See, our master didn't like us to have much 'ligion, said it made us lag in our work. He jest wanted us to be Catholicses on Sundays and go to mass and not study 'bout nothin' like that on week days. He didn't want us shoutin' and moanin' all day'-long, but you gotta shout and you gotta moan if you wants to be saved.[20]

The slaves clearly craved the affirmation and promise of their religion. It would be a mistake, however, to see this urge as exclusively otherworldly. When Thomas Wentworth Higginson observed that the spirituals exhibited "nothing but patience for this life,—nothing but triumph in the next," he, and later observers who elaborated upon this judgment, were indulging in hyperbole. Although Jesus was ubiquitous in the spirituals, it was not invariably the Jesus of the New Testament of whom the slaves sang, but frequently a Jesus transformed into an Old Testament warrior: "Mass' Jesus" who engaged in personal combat with the Devil; "King Jesus" seated on a milk-white horse with sword and shield in hand. "Ride on, King Jesus," "Ride on, conquering King," "The God I serve is a man of war," the slaves sang.[21] This transformation of Jesus is symptomatic of the slaves' selectivity in choosing those parts of the Bible which were to serve as the basis for their religious consciousness. Howard Thurman, a Negro minister who as a boy had the duty of reading the Bible to his grandmother, was perplexed by her refusal to allow him to read from the Epistles of Paul.

> When at length I asked the reason, she told me that during the days of slavery, the minister (white) on the plantation was always preaching from the Pauline letters—"Slaves, be obedient to your masters," etc. "I vowed to myself," she said, "that if freedom ever came and I learned to read, I would never read that part of the Bible!"[22]

Nor, apparently, did this part of the Scriptures ever constitute a vital element in slave songs or sermons. The emphasis of the spirituals, as Higginson himself noted, was upon the Old Testament and the exploits of the Hebrew children. It is important that Daniel and David and Joshua and Jonah and Moses and Noah, all of whom fill the lines of the spirituals, were delivered in *this* world and delivered in ways which struck the imagination of the slaves. Over and over their songs dwelt upon the spectacle of the Red Sea opening to allow the Hebrew slaves past before inundating the mighty armies of the Pharaoh. They lingered delightedly upon the image of little David humbling the great Goliath with a stone—a pretechnological victory which post-bellum Negroes were to expand upon in their songs of John Henry. They retold in endless variation the stories of the blind and humbled Samson bringing down the mansions of his conquerors; of the ridiculed Noah patiently building the ark which would deliver him from the doom of a mocking world; of the timid Jonah attaining freedom from his confinement through faith. The similarity of these tales to the situation of the slave was too clear for him not to see it; too clear for us to believe that the songs had no worldly content for the black man in bondage. "O my Lord delivered Daniel," the slaves observed, and responded logically: "O why not deliver me, too?"

> *He delivered Daniel from de lion's den,*
> *Jonah from de belly ob de whale*
> *And de Hebrew children from de fiery furnace,*
> *And why not every man?*[24]

These lines state as clearly as anything can the manner in which the sacred world of the slaves was able to fuse the precedents of the past, the conditions of the present, and the promise of the future into one connected reality. In this report there was always a latent and symbolic element of protest in the slave's religious songs which frequently became overt and explicit. Frederick Douglass asserted that for him and many of his fellow slaves the song. "O Canaan, sweet Canaan./I am bound for the land of Canaan," symbolized "something more than a hope of reaching heaven. We meant to reach the *North*, and the North was our Canaan," and he wrote that the lines of another spiritual, "Run to Jesus, shun the danger./I don't expect to stay much longer here," had a double meaning which first suggested to him the thought of escaping from slavery.[25] Similarly, when the black troops in Higginson's regiment sang:

> *We'll soon be free, [three times]*
> *When de Lord will call us home.*

a young drummer boy explained to him, "Dey think *de Lord* mean for say *de Yankees.*"[26] Nor is there any reason to doubt that slaves could have used their songs as a means of secret communication. An ex-slave told Lydia Parrish that when he and his fellow slaves "suspicioned" that one of their number was telling tales to the driver, they would sing lines like the following while working in the field:

> *O Judyas he wuz a'ceitful man*
> *He went an' betray a mos' innocen' man.*
> *Fo' thirty pieces a silver dat it wuz done*
> *He went in de woods an' e' self he hung.*[27]

And it is possible, as many writers have argued, that such spirituals as the commonly heard "Steal away, steal away, steal away to Jesus!" were used as explicit calls to secret meetings.

But, it is not necessary to invest the spirituals with a secular function only at the price of divesting them of their religious content, as Miles Mark Fisher has done.[28] While we may make such clear-cut distinctions, I have tried to show that the slaves did not. For them religion never constituted a simple escape from this world, because their conception of the world was more expansive than modern man's. Nowhere is this better illustrated than during the Civil War itself. While the war gave rise to such new spirituals as "Before I'd be a slave/I'd be buried in my grave,/And go home to my Lord and be saved!" or the popular "Many thousand Go," with its jubilant rejection of all the facets of slave life—"No more peck o' corn for me, . . . No more driver's lash for me, . . . No more pint o' salt for me, . . . No more hundred lash for me, . . . No more mistress' call for me"[29]—the important thing was not that large numbers of slaves now could create new songs which openly expressed their views of slavery: that was to be expected.

More significant was the ease with which their old songs fit their new situation. With so much of their inspiration drawn from the events of the Old Testament and the Book of Revelation, the slaves had long sung of wars, of battles, of the Army of the Lord, of Soldiers of the Cross, of trumpets summoning the faithful, of vanquishing the hosts of evil. These songs especially were, as Higginson put it, "available for camp purposes with very little strain upon their symbolism." "We'll cross de mighty river," his troops sang while marching or rowing,

> *We'll cross de danger water, . . .*
> *O Pharaoh's army drownded!*
> *My army cross over.*

"O blow your trumpet, Gabriel," they sang,

> *Blow your trumpet louder;*
> *And I want dat trumpet to blow me home*
> *To my new Jerusalem.*

But they also found their less overtly militant songs quite as appropriate to warfare. Their most popular and effective marching song was:

> *Jesus call you, Go in de wilderness,*
> *   Go in de wilderness, go in de wilderness,*
> *Jesus call you. Go in de wilderness*
> *   To wait upon de Lord.*[30]

Black Union soldiers found it no more incongruous to accompany their fight for freedom with the sacred songs of their bondage than thay had found it inappropriate as slaves to sing their spirituals while picking cotton or shucking corn. Their religious songs, like their religion itself, was of this world as well as the next.

Slave songs by themselves, of course, do not present us with a definitive key to the life and mind of the slave. They have to be seen within the context of the slave's situation and examined alongside such other cultural materials as folk tales. But slave songs do indicate the need to rethink a number of assumptions that have shaped recent interpretations of slavery, such as the assumption that because slavery eroded the linguistic and institutional side of African life it wiped out almost all the more fundamental aspects of African culture. Culture, certainly, is more than merely the sum total of institutions and language. It is also expressed by something less tangible, which the anthropologist Robert Redfield has called "style of life." Peoples as different as the Lapp and the Bedouin, Redfield has argued, with diverse languages, religions, customs, and institutions, may still share an emphasis on certain virtues and ideals, certain manners of independence and hospitality, general ways of looking upon the world, which give them a similar life style.[31] This argument applies to the West African cultures from which the slaves came. Though they varied widely in language, institutions, gods, and familial patterns, they shared a fundamental outlook toward the past, present, and future and common means of cultural expression which could well have constituted the basis of a sense of community and identity capable of surviving the impact of slavery.

Slave songs present us with abundant evidence that in the structure of their music and dance, in the uses to which music was put, in the survival of the oral tradition, in the retention of such practices as spirit possession which often accompanied the creation of spirituals, and in the ways in which the slaves expressed their new religion, important elements of their shared African heritage remained alive not just as quaint cultural vestiges but as vitally creative elements of slave culture. This could never have happened if slavery was, as Professor Elkins maintains, a system which so completely closed in around the slave, so totally penetrated his personality structure as to infantalize him and reduce him to a kind of *tabula rasa* upon which the white man could write what he chose.[32]

Slave songs provide us with the beginnings of a very different kind of hypothesis: that the preliterate, premodern Africans, with their sacred world view, were so imperfectly acculturated into the secular American society into which they were thrust, were so completely denied access to the ideology and dreams which formed the core of the consciousness of other Americans, that they were forced to fall back upon the only cultural frames of reference that made any sense to them and gave them any feeling of security. I use the word "forced" advisedly. Even if the slaves had had the opportunity to enter fully into the life of the larger society, they might still have chosen to retain and perpetuate certain elements of their African heritage. But the point is that they really had no choice. True acculturation was denied to most slaves. The alternatives were either to remain in a state of cultural limbo, divested of the old cultural patterns but not allowed to adopt those of their new homeland—which in the long run is no alternative at all—or to cling to as many as possible of the old ways of thinking and acting. The slaves' oral tradition, their music, and their religious outlook served this latter function and constituted a cultural refuge at least potentially capable of protecting their personalities from some of the worst ravages of the slave system.

The argument of Professors Tannenbaum and Elkins that the Protestant churches in the United States did not act as a buffer between the slave and his master is persuasive enough, but it betrays a modern preoccupation with purely institutional arrangements.[33] Religion is more than an institution, and because Protestant churches failed to protect the slave's inner being from the incursions of the slave system, it does not follow that the spiritual message of Protestantism failed as well. Slave songs are a testament to the ways in which Christianity provided slaves with the precedents, heroes, and future promise that allowed them to transcend the purely temporal bonds of the Peculiar Institution.

Historians have frequently failed to perceive the full importance of this because they have not taken the slave's religiosity seriously enough. A people cannot create a music as forceful and striking as slave music out of a mere uninternalized anodyne. Those who have argued that Negroes did not oppose slavery in any meaningful way are writing from a modern, political context. What they really mean is that the slaves found no *political* means to oppose slavery. But slaves, to borrow Professor Hobsbawm's term, were prepolitical beings in a prepolitical situation.[34] Within their frame of reference there were other—and from the point of view of personality development, not necessarily less effective—means of escape and opposition. If mid-twentieth-century historians have difficulty perceiving the sacred universe created by slaves as a serious alternative to the societal system created by southern slave holders, the problem may be the historians' and not the slaves'.

Above all, the study of the slave songs forces the historian to move out of his own culture, in which music plays a peripheral role, and offers him the opportunity to understand the ways in which black slaves were able to perpetuate much of the centrality and functional importance that music had for their African ancestors. In the concluding lines of his perceptive study of primitive song, C. M. Bowra has written:

> Primitive song is indispensable to those who practice it. . . . they cannot do without song, which both formulates and answers their nagging questions, enables them to pursue action with zest and confidence, brings them into touch with gods and spirits, and makes them feel

less strange in the natural world. . . . it gives to them a solid centre in what otherwise would be almost chaos, and a continuity in their being, which would too easily dissolve before the calls of the implacable present . . . through its words men, who might otherwise give in to the malice of circumstances, find their old powers revived or new powers stirring in them, and through these life itself is sustained and renewed and fulfilled.[35]

This, I think, sums up concisely the function of song for the slave. Without a general understanding of that function, without a specific understanding of the content and meaning of slave song, there can be no full comprehension of the effects of slavery upon the slave or the meaning of the society from which slaves emerged at emancipation.

NOTES

1. Lucy McKim, "Songs of the Port Royal Contrabands," *Dwight's Journal of Music*, XXII (November 8,1862), 255.
2. Mircea Eliade, *The Sacred and the Profane* (New York, 1961), Chaps. 2, 4, and *passim*. For the similarity of Eliade's concept to the world view of West Africa, see W. E. Abraham, *The Mind of Africa* (London, 1962), Chap. 2, and R. S. Rattray, *Religion and Art in Ashanti* (Oxford, 1927).
3. Paul Radin, "Status, Phantasy, and the Christian Dogma," in Social Science Institute, Fisk University, *God Struck Me Dead: Religious Conversion Experiences and Autobiographies of Negro Ex-Slaves* (Nashville, 1945, unpublished typescript).
4. Stanley Elkins, *Slavery* (Chicago, 1959), 136.
5. William Francis Allen, Charles Pickford Ware, and Lucy McKim Garrison, compilers, *Slave Songs of the United States* (New York, 1867, Oak Publications ed., 1965), 33-34, 105; William E. Barton, *Old Plantation Hymns: A Collection of Hitherto Unpublished Melodies of the Slave and the Freedmen* (Boston, 1899), 30.
6. Allen, *et al*, *Slave Songs of the United States*, 47.
7. Barton, *Old Plantation Hymns*, 19.
8. J. B. T. Marsh, *The Story of the Jubilee Singers; With Their Songs* (Boston, 1880), 132.
9. Thomas P. Fenner, compiler, *Religious Folk Songs of the Negro as Sung on the Plantations* (Hampton, Virginia, 1909, orig. pub. 1874), 162; E. A. McIlhenny, *Befo' De War Spirituals: Words and Melodies* (Boston, 1933), 39.
10. Barton, *Old Plantation Hymns*, 15; Howard W. Odum and Guy B. Johnson, *The Negro and His Songs* (Hatboro, Penn., 1964, orig. pub. 1925), 33-34; for a vivid description of the "shout" see *The Nation*, May 30, 1867,

432-433; see also Lydia Parrish, *Slave Songs of the Georgia Sea Islands* (Hatboro, Penn., 1965, orig. pub. 1942), Chap. 3.

11. For examples of songs of this nature, see Fenner, *Religious Folk Songs of the Negro*, 8, 63-65; Marsh, *The Story of the Jubilee Singers*, 240-241; Thomas Wentworth Higginson, *Army Life in a Black Regiment* (Beacon Press ed., Boston, 1962, orig. pub. 1869), 205; Allen *et al*, *Slave Songs of the United States*, 91, 100; Natalie Curtis Burlin, *Negro Folk-Songs* (New York, 1918-1919), I, 37-42.

12. Allen, *et al*, *Slave Songs of the United States*, 32-33.

13. Ibid., 30-31; Burlin, *Negro Folk-Songs*, II, 8-9; Fenner, *Religious Folk Songs of the Negro*, 12.

14. Allen, et al, *Slave Songs of the United States*, 128-129; Fenner, *Religious Folk Songs of the Negro*, 127; Barton, *Old Plantation Hymns*, 26.

15. Allen, et al, *Slave Songs of the United States*, 70, 102-103, 147; Barton, *Old Plantation Hymns*, 9, 17-18, 24; Marsh, *The Story of the Jubilee Singers*, 133, 167; Odum and Johnson, *The Negro and His Songs*, 35.

16. Allen, *et al*, *Slave Songs of the United States*, 102-103.

17. Mary Allen Grissom, compiler, *The Negro Sings a New Heaven* (Chapel Hill, 1930), 73.

18. Marsh, *The Story of the Jubilee Singers*, 179, 186; Allen, *et al*, *Slave Songs of the United States*, 40-41, 44, 146; Barton, *Old Plantation Hymns*, 30.

19. McIlhenny, *Befo' De War Spirituals*, 31.

20. *Gumbo Ya-Ya: A Collection of Louisiana Folk Tales*, compiled by Lyle Saxon, Edward Dreyer, and Robert Tallant from materials gathered by workers of the WPA, Louisiana Writer's Project (Boston, 1945), 242.

21. For examples, Allen, *et al*, *Slave Songs of the United States*, 40-41, 82, 97, 106-108; Marsh, *The Story of the Jubilee Singers*, 168, 203; Burlin, *Negro Folk-Songs*, II, 8-9; Howard Thurman, *Deep River* (New York, 1945), 19-21.

22. Thurman, *Deep River*, 16-17.

23. Higginson, *Army Life in a Black Regiment*, 202-205. Many of those northerners who came to the South to "uplift" the freedmen were deeply disturbed at the Old Testament emphasis of their religion. H. G. Spaulding complained that the ex-slaves needed to be introduced to "the light and warmth of the Gospel," and reported that a Union army officer told him: "Those people had enough of the Old Testament thrown at their heads under slavery. Now give them the glorious utterances and practical teachings of the Great Master." Spaulding, "Under the Palmetto," reprinted in Bruce Jackson (ed.), *The Negro and His Folklore in Nineteenth-Century Periodicals* (Austin, 1967), 66.

24. Allen, *et al*, *Slave Songs of the United States*, 148; Fenner, *Religious Folk Songs of the Negro*, 21; Marsh, *The Story of the Jubilee Singers*, 134-135; McIlhenny, *Befo' De War Spirituals*, 248-249.

25. *Life and Times of Frederick Douglass* (rev. ed., 1892, Collier Books ed., 1962), 159-160; Marsh, *The Story of the Jubilee Singers*, 188.

26. Higginson, *Army Life in a Black Regiment*, 217.

27. Parrish, *Slave Songs of the Georgia Sea Islands*, 247.
28. "Actually, not one spiritual in its primary form reflected interest in any-thing other than a full life here and now." Miles Mark Fisher, *Negro Slave Songs in the United States* (New York, 1963, orig. pub. 1953), 137.
29. Barton, *Old Plantation Hymns*, 25; Allen, *et al*, *Slave Songs of the United States*, 94; James Miller McKim, "Negro Songs," *Dwight's Journal of Music*, XXI (August 9, 1862), 149.
30. Higginson, *Army Life in a Black Regiment*, 201-202, 211-212.
31. Robert Redfield, *The Primitive World and Its Transformations* (Ithaca, 1953), 51-53.
32. Elkins, *Slavery*, Chap. 3.
33. *Ibid.*, Chap. 2; Frank Tannenbaum, *Slave and Citizen* (New York, 1946).
34. E. J. Hobsbawm, *Primitive Rebels* (New York, 1959), Chap. 1.
35. C. M. Bowra, *Primitive Song* (London, 1962), 285-286.

The Black Family
in
Slavery and Freedom

HERBERT GUTMAN

In this essay Herbert Gutman, author of the widely-acclaimed *The Black Family in Slavery and Freedom, 1750-1925* (1976), studies the *last* generation of slaves. He disputes the once conventional wisdom that the breakup of the slave family by sale debilitated the black family thereafter. To be sure, slave sales were distressingly frequent and disruptive, and even in freedom the black family suffered assaults from whites and impersonal economic forces. What impressed Gutman in all this was the resiliency of the black family under trying conditions. Whether on plantations or in towns, blacks fought to keep their families intact. Slaves knew who they were through their families, as the attempts to locate lost relatives after the war attested. Slaves ordered their world in family terms. Monogamous units formed the basis of slave society, but elaborate, extended kinship ties bound the separate units together into a community that extended over time and place. How did the experience of the last generation of slaves reflect the slaves' adaptive qualities over time? In what ways did the slave family adjust to the harshness of bondage? What does the length of slave marriages show about slave family arrangements and values? How did young slaves learn about proper family arrangements? Compare

Reprinted from Herbert G. Gutman, *The Black Family in Slavery and Freedom, 1750-1925* (New York: Pantheon, 1976) pp. 7-9, 14, 15-26, 27-28, 31-34, without notes and tables, by permission of the author. Copyright © 1976 by Herbert G. Gutman.

Gutman with Thomas Webber in the next selection on this question. How autonomous was the black family? What does the freedmen's quest for legal documentation of their marital status after the war suggest about their acceptance of white norms? What does the immediate postwar experience of black women show about the prevailing moral code among slaves? What are the limitations of studying the last generation of slaves to draw conclusions about the changing history of slaves?

The recovery of records of viable Afro-American families and kin networks during and after slavery makes it possible to begin a long overdue examination of how there developed among black Americans a culture shaped by the special ways in which they adapted first to the harshness of initial enslavement, then to the severe dislocations associated with the physical transfer of hundreds of thousands of Upper South slaves to the Lower South between 1790 and 1860, and later to legal freedom in the rural and urban South and in the urban North prior to 1930. The sociologist T. B. Bottomore reminds us that "the family transmits values which are determined elsewhere; it is an agent, not a principal." But for it to be an "agent," there must be links between generations of different families. Without them, it is difficult for a culture to be transmitted over time, and members of developing social classes cannot adapt to changing external circumstances. That is so for slaves and nonslaves.

The family condition and familial beliefs of some Virginia, North Carolina, Mississippi, Louisiana, Tennessee and Kentucky Afro-Americans between 1863 and 1866—*the last slave generation*—are examined first. Who these ex-slaves were and the types of families they lived in between 1863 and 1866 pose questions about who they had been in the half century preceding the general emancipation and who they would become in the half century following it. Evidence about them in 1865 provides important clues to who their slave grandparents had been in 1815 (before the rapid spread of slavery from the Upper to the Lower South) and who their grandchildren would be in 1915 (at the beginning of the twentieth-century migration of rural southern blacks to northern cities). The emancipation freed the slaves not only of their owners but also of the constraints that had limited their ability to act upon their slave beliefs, and their behavior during and shortly after the Civil War reveals aspects of that earlier belief system otherwise difficult for the historian to discern. Early-twentieth-century historians and social scientists suggested such continuities, but either their racial beliefs or the flawed sociohistorical "models" they used to explain lower-class behavior over time led them to stress "continuities" that had no relationship at all to the behavior of ordinary ex-slaves.

No one better illustrates this misdirected emphasis than the sociologist E. Franklin Frazier. Frazier, of course, was not a racist and vigorously combatted the racial scholarship that dominated early-twentieth-century historical and social-science writings. But he underestimated the adaptive capacities of slaves and ex-slaves and therefore wrote that their families, "at best an accommodation to the slave order, went to pieces in the general breakup of the plantation system." He had the ex-slave laborer and field hand in mind when he asked:

> What authority was there to take the place of the master's in regulating sex relations and maintaining the permanency of marital ties? Where could the Negro father look for sanctions of his authority in family relations which had scarcely existed in the past? Were the affectional bonds between mother and child and the solidarity of feeling and sentiment between man and wife strong enough to withstand the disorganizing effects of freedom? In the absence of family traditions and public opinion, what restraint was there upon individual impulses unleashed in these disordered times? To what extent during slavery had the members of slave families developed common interests and common purposes capable of supporting the more or less loose ties of sympathy between those of the same blood or household?

The "crisis" accompanying emancipation "tended to destroy all traditional ways of thinking." "Promiscuous sexual relations and constant changing of partners became the rule" among "demoralized blacks," and the rest hardly fared better. "When the yoke of slavery was lifted," he wrote, "the drifting masses were left without any restraint upon their vagrant impulses and wild desires. The old intimacy between master and slave, upon which the moral order of the slave regime had rested, was destroyed forever." Frazier's influential writings paradoxically fed the racist scholarship he attacked. Frazier's error was not that he exaggerated the social crisis accompanying emancipation but his belief that the "moral order of the slave regime . . . rested" on "the old intimacy between master and slave." Some slaves experienced such intimacies, but neither the beliefs and behavior of most slaves nor their familial arrangements depended upon so fragile a bond. . . .

Evidence of long marriages is found in all slave social settings in the decades preceding the Civil War. Young slaves learned about marital and family roles from whites and free blacks, but they also had the opportunity to learn from other slaves, a fact confirmed by the nearly twenty thousand North Carolina ex-slaves in seventeen different counties who registered slave marriages with county clerks and justices of the peace in the spring of 1866 after the North Carolina legislature had ordered the registration of all continuing slave marriages. . . . Drawn from just a few counties, the *registrants* totaled about 14 percent of North Carolina's *entire* 1860 adult slave population.

Nearly similar percentages of slave couples everywhere reported long-lasting marriages. About one in four couples had lived together between ten and nineteen years, and slightly more than one in five at least twenty years. Nearly one in ten registrants recorded marriages that had lasted thirty or more years. Insignificant percentage-point differences existed between the counties. . . . Settled slave marriage "models" and domestic arrangements existed in all types of slave settings. The uniformities reported described only the length of slave marriages and did not indicate these registrants had shared similiar slave experiences. That is the essential point. How these slaves had lived can be approximated very crudely by examining five different measures of dissimilarity: the degree of urbanization, the sex ratio, the density of the slave population, access to free blacks, and patterns of slave ownership that suggest community and social structure. . . . We consider only the distribution of slaves in 1860, a measure that allows for a comparison between the North Carolina blacks and *Lower South* slaves in settings where the plantation system and the social structure associated with it were much more common than in North Carolina.

Most North Carolina slaves in 1860 were not a part of the plantation economy, but registrants in the eight plantation counties (Bertie, Edgecombe, Franklin, Halifax, Johnston, Nash, Richmond, and Warren) shared a common slave setting with blacks living on large Lower South and South Carolina plantations. . . . The typical North Carolina plantation county couple registering a marriage in 1866 almost surely lived in densely black areas and worked the land as field hands or common laborers. Long-lasting marriages had existed among them just as long-lasting slave marriages were found among Mississippi, Louisiana, and Alabama slaves during and right after the Civil War.

The North Carolina registrants also showed that a special relationship did not exist between long slave marriages and the large plantation. Couples living in predominantly farm settings and in the county with North Carolina's largest city registered long marriages in the same proportion as men and women living in predominantly plantation counties. A plantation setting therefore was not a prerequisite for a long slave marriage.

Much in their social experience went unreported when these nearly nineteen thousand ex-slaves registered marriages, but the little they revealed—the length of their marriages—uncovers an aspect of slave life essential to comprehending slave behavior and belief prior to and just after the emancipation. These men and women had not reported that North Carolina slaves lived in "stable " marriages or families. Nor did what they had experienced mean that the forcible breakup of marriages and families had occurred infrequently. . . . Instead, because the registers showed that settled slave marriages existed in very diverse social circumstances, it meant that young slaves everywhere learned from other slaves about marital and familial obligations and about managing difficult daily social realities. Adult slaves in long marriages were direct "models," making it possible to pass on *slave* conceptions of marital, familial, and kin obligation from generation to generation. The domestic arrangements visibly accessible to young slaves were not just those of shattered slave families and the more secure families of owners, other whites, and free blacks. How married slaves dealt with family life and social existence over time taught them much more than what they could learn from better-advantaged whites or from scattered communities of free blacks.

Although these North Carolina and Virginia ex-slaves revealed that many ordinary Upper South slaves, including plantation field hands, had lived in long marriages, that record told little about how the decisions of slaveowners affected slave marriages. Testimony detailing how frequently sale had disrupted their marriages, however, comes from Mississippi and northern Louisiana ex-slaves. In March 1864, John Eaton, the Superintendent of Contrabands in the Department of the Tennessee and Arkansas, issued a military edict (Special Order 15) instructing Union Army clergy to "solemnize the rite of marriage among Freedmen," give such blacks "neat" marriage certificates, and record these marriages in registration books. Even before this order, northern missionaries had pressed legal marriage upon contraband Mississippi Valley blacks within the Union Army lines. Special Order 15 did not require that married slaves renew their ties before an army clergyman, and those who did so acted voluntarily. Ex-slaves in and near Davis Bend, Vicksburg, and Natchez, Mississippi, registered 4627 marriages. Officiating clergy did not charge fees, but some blacks paid them with rewards such as a silver dime, some postal currency, "half a dime," and a sweet potato (this from a woman who "begged" a chaplain to take "a small token" for what had been done "for her and her family"). . . .

The officiating clergy gathered unusual social and demographic data from those registering slave marriages or marrying for the first time. Nearly all reported their age, their color, the color of each of their parents, their earlier slave marriages, the reasons these marriages had ended, and the length of these earlier marriages. Most registrants described themselves *and their parents* as "black." They apparently had a choice or, at least, the officiating clergy made subtle color distinctions among them, including "black," "brown," "yellow," "coffee," "mulatto," "white," and "¼ white." Each registrant also gave the color of his or her parents, a designation that could not have been made by the registrars. The "fractional" designations used to describe many parents also suggested that the registrants knew a great deal about their grandparents. Overall, more than three in five said that both parents were "black." These men and women refute the suggestion by some historians that slave marriages bore a special relationship to mixed "blood." Six registrants claimed a white mother, and about one in twenty-five (3.7 percent) a white father. Thirty-seven percent, however, admitted to "mixed color," so that more than one in three of these more than nine thousand Lower South slaves traced white ancestry to racial intermixture that had occurred among their grandparents and great-grandparents, mixing that had mostly taken place in thè eighteenth century. Unless large numbers of the registrants had French or Spanish grandparents, these white and black grandparents and great-grandparents had lived in the Upper South. . . .

Their ages indicate that these Mississippi and northern Louisiana registrants combined two, and perhaps three, generations of distinct slave experiences. A high percentage of all registrants were men and especially women not yet thirty years old: nearly two in five men and slightly more than half of all women. All these people had been born after 1835 and therefore had been born at the time of the interregional transfer of Upper South slaves to the Lower South. If they had had contact with Upper South slavery, it was probably as children or from what they had learned from parents and other older blacks. About one in six registrants were at least fifty years old. These men and women had been born before Mississippi entered the Union as a state (1817), and many among them had probably grown up as Upper South and border-state slaves. Some had been born in the eighteenth century. Four men were at least ninety years old, and a woman, separated by force from an earlier husband with whom she had lived for forty-five years, claimed a full century of life. Natchez officials registered the marriage of a one-hundred-year-old husband and his seventy-eight-year-old wife. When Jacob Wiley and Phoebe Tanner registered their marriage in Davis Bend, he was ninety-three and she was eighty. Life experiences that encompassed the spread of slavery and the physical movement of black men and women from the Upper to the Lower South had not convinced these elderly ex-slaves that legal marriage was a privilege belonging only to the owning class and to other whites.

Registrants gave the clergy information about earlier slave marriages (data examined in detail in Chapter 4), and their testimony unfolded a grim record. One in four marriages registered in 1864-1865 involved one or two persons separated by force from a spouse in an earlier marriage. In marriages in which either partner was at least forty years old in 1864-1865, the percentage in which one or both had experienced an earlier marriage broken by force rose to 35 percent. Among people that old, seven in ten marriages registered in 1864-1865 included one or two people who had been married earlier. Nearly as many of these 1864-1865 marriages included a prior marriage broken by force as broken by death, a more severe indictment of the cost slavery had exacted from Afro-Americans than the most telling words of Frederick Douglass, not to mention William Lloyd Garrison and Harriet Beecher Stowe.

The registration of so many slave marriages by these Mississippi and northern Louisiana blacks impressed Union Army officers among them. Thomas Calahan, who commanded black Mississippi troops, said they had "an almost universal anxiety . . . to abide first connections. Many, both men and women with whom I am acquainted, whose wives or husbands the rebels have driven off, firmly refuse to form new connections, and declare their purpose to keep faith to absent ones." Neither John Eaton nor Joseph Warren, his chief associate, idealized these marriage renewals. "It is not pretended," remarked Eaton, "that all marriages that have taken place were well advised, or will be happy, or faithfully observed. When marriages among whites shall all prove so, without exception, it will be time to look for such a happy state among the blacks." A year after Special Order 15 had been instituted,

Warren said, "I will only remark that the ill-natured predictions of many persons have not been fulfilled. Marriage is not treated as a light matter." A "few" marriages had ended because of the "inconstancy of the partners, " but it put Warren "utterly out of patience to hear people . . . say it is folly to marry blacks, because they will be fickle, and then quote a single case of unfaithfulness . . . in proof of their monstrous proposition. Would they recommend that the colored people herd together like beasts . . . [and] that marriage be abolished among white people because there are some cases of discontent and fickleness among us?" Their behavior convinced Warren to put aside talk of "the incapacity of the race"; "so many" were "able to 'take care of themselves' without guardianship or tutelage." How the ex-slaves responded to Special Order 15 convinced Eaton that their families had been forcibly broken much more frequently than he had believed, but their attachment to their families impressed him: "Many have said, 'They do not feel these things as we do.' This is utterly false. . . . They are a race of peculiarly keen feelings and domestic tendencies, and they have fewer means of withdrawing their minds from their griefs than we have."

The concern of Mississippi and northern Louisiana ex-slaves serving in the Union Army for their families shows that Eaton and these others had not been deceived. Black Vicksburg soldiers "complained bitterly" in early 1864 that their wives had been "taken away from them and sent they knew not to what camp or plantation." Other black troops found four hundred "exceedingly destitute" ex-slaves, some kin among them, near Videlia, Louisiana, and threatened to desert. "We are concluding to leave our regiment," Laura Haviland, a northern relief worker among them, overheard one ex-slave say, "and build something to shelter and house our children." After she and other sympathetic whites promised relief, the threats subsided. But the soldiers stayed a few days to see what would happen. Other ex-slaves, recruited to garrison a post near Milliken's Bend, were sent to Waterproof. Their families had gathered near Milliken's Bend. "The men complained bitterly," said a supervising white, "about the way they have been treated by being taken away from their wives." They would "submit to the necessity of the occasion provided they can feel that their wives are cared for." But according to Thomas Knox, a New York *Herald* correspondent who had leased a wartime Mississippi plantation, "their affection for their wives and children could not be overcome at once." Their complaints at first were "silenced." A few weeks later, a few soldiers quit Waterproof and made their way back to Milliken's Bend. They ended in the guardhouse, but "others followed their example, and for a while the camp was in a disturbed condition." Desertions occurred daily. "All intended to return to the post after making a brief visit to their families," said Knox. "Most . . . would request their comrades to notify their captains that they would only be absent a short time. Two, who succeeded in eluding pursuit, made their appearance one morning as if nothing had happened and assured their officers that others would shortly be back again."

Such concern for their families was most decisively revealed by ex-slave soldiers in and near Natchez in early April 1864, a few weeks after Special Order 15 went into effect. Treasury Department officials had arranged for the leasing of abandoned plantations to northerners, and some Union Army officers tried to force ex-slaves, who had crowded Natchez and a refugee camp nearby, to labor for the lessees. Late in March, the Natchez army surgeon and chief health officer A. W. Kelly, supported by J. W. Tuttle, the city's military commander, announced that *"idle ne-groes"* posed a "serious danger" to public health and threatened to spread "the most *loathsome* and *malignant* diseases" among Union Army soldiers. After April 1, only ex-slaves employed by *"some responsible white person* in some legitimate business" and living with their employers could remain in Natchez. Ex-slaves could no longer rent premises, and whites employing them needed Kelly's approval. The protests of a few northern schoolteachers and missionaries led by S. G. Wright, who called Kelly "an inhuman monster" and *"a Fiend,"*had no effect. Tuttle rejected their formal complaints, threatened them with punitive action, and said they "appear to think that colored men have a great many more rights than white men." Kelly's edict was enforced. "Mothers," said Wright, "came running to us *weeping*, begging us to go & plead their cause." Parents were separated from their children, and husbands and wives from one another. . . . "Scores" of women and children were moved from Natchez and left "shelterless and destitute" across the Mississippi River in Louisiana. The angered and frustrated Wright pleaded with northern associates to press for intervention by the Secretary of War. "What," Wright reported the ex-slaves as asking, "has the [Emancipation] Proclamation really done for us if military officers are to have the power to drive us from our quiet homes into the streets, separate husband wife parents & children &c?"

Ex-slave Mississippi soldiers checked Kelly's abusive edict. "The colored soldier," the missionaries had warned Tuttle, "hearing that his mother or his wife had been driven from her quiet and comfortable home, simply because she supported herself and was not dependent upon some white person, may feel less inclined to hazard his life in the cause of his country now struggling for *its* life." Many evicted and abused women had husbands in army camps near Natchez, and some went to their husbands "for protection." "I heard colored soldiers yesterday in their madness swear desperately that they would have *revenge. And they will,"* Wright privately confided to a northern friend. "I tremble as do many of the officers in the colored regiments, when I witness such expressions and conduct of the soldiers," he added, fearing "blood equalling the day of vengeance in the island of Hayti." The ex-slave soldiers acted decisively. The first night after Kelly's edict was enforced, fifteen deserted their regiments. Three days later, other ex-slave soldiers, their exact number unknown, told their commanding officer that "they could no longer endure the trial of seeing their wives and children driven into the streets, and if he would not at once interfere and protect them they should *positively* do it themselves." Their threat was understood, and the officer released some women and children kept by Kelly. A few days later, Kelly's "health ordinance" was modified. "The colored troops here arose," Wright privately enthused, "& even Dr. Kelly caved in...." A few weeks later, Kelly and Tuttle were relieved of their command. "The people all breathe easier," said Wright.

The Natchez ex-slave women were far more fortunate than ex-slave women living in Memphis in the spring of 1866. A few days after the disarming and discharge of Union Army black soldiers in Fort Pickering nearby, Memphis was the scene of a murderous riot. Local whites, the mostly Irish police prominent among them, killed forty-six blacks, wounded at least seventy others, robbed about one hundred ex-slaves, and burned at least ninety black dwellings, including twelve schoolhouses and four churches. Whites also raped at least five ex-slaves and sexually insulted two others, facts revealed by the testimony these women and other witnesses, including a few whites, gave to a congressional committee. What gives such testimony its importance is not merely the pain and insult experienced by these women. It is rather the willingness of recent slaves to expose their suffering in public so soon after the Civil War's end.

Four of the seven women, including two of those raped, were unmarried. Asked if she was married, the washerwoman Elvira Walker said, "A man boards with me; he is not my husband; he sleeps in the same room." She was alone the night rioters robbed her room. One "put his hands into my bosom," she told the congressional investigators. "I tried to stop him, and he knocked down my hands with his pistol." . . . No one interceded to assist Frances Thompson and Lucy Smith. The two lived together. A Maryland slave by birth, Thompson, the older of the two, was crippled by a cancer in her foot and walked with crutches. She labored as a washerwoman. A Memphis native, Lucy Smith was seventeen years old. Seven men, including two police officers, broke into their place, demanded and were fed supper, robbed Frances Thompson of one hundred dollars and four "nice" dresses, took another two hundred dollars the older woman was keeping for a friend, and raped both women. The older of the two testified:

> When they had eaten supper, they said they wanted some woman to sleep with. I said we were not that sort of woman, and they must go. They said "that didn't make a damned bit of difference." One of them then laid hold of me and hit me on the side of my face, holding my throat, choked me. Lucy tried to get out of the window, when one of them knocked her down and choked her. They drew their pistols and said they would shoot us and fire the house if we did not let them have their way with us. All seven of them violated us two. Four of them had to do with me, and the rest with Lucy. . . .

Lucy Smith differed slightly in telling what had happened: "After the first man had connexion with me, another got hold of me and tried to violate me, but I was so bad he did not. He gave me a lick with his fist and said I was so damned near dead he would not have anything to do with me. . . . I bled from what the first man done to me. . . . I was injured right smart. " Black physicians later attended the two women. Lucy Smith was in bed for two weeks, and the older woman "lay for three days with a hot, burning fever."

The Memphis rioters had their way for many reasons, including the unwillingness of Union Army officers to let black soldiers nearby protect their families. Two days before the riot, the soldiers had been disarmed. Some kept revolvers, but none had heavier weapons. After the riot began, white soldiers guarded stacked weapons. A white army captain, who later told the congressional committee that he "sympathized with the colored people and . . . was sorry that the men could not get arms . . . to defend their wives and children," said that on the first night of the rioting "many of the colored soldiers wanted their arms." "I heard them say we must have our arms," testified Thomas J. Durnin, and "some twelve or fifteen" rushed the building where the arms were stored. "I gave the order to fire," Durnin remembered. "The men had their bayonets fixed, but the colored soldiers retreated at the first fire." The ex-slaves, Durnin said, "regretted that they had returned their arms" and were "very much excited and begging to have their arms that they might defend the women and children." Despite an order to keep the men in the fort, about one hundred apparently unarmed soldiers "all broke out at once" the first night. The next day, the Memphis mayor, advised by an army officer that if the men got an idea of the disorders nearby "it would be impossible to keep them in," promised the black ex-soldiers that their homes would not be burned and their families protected. An officer reminded the assembled blacks that they "had no arms." The soldiers spoke out, saying they had heard whites "were burning the houses and murdering their wives and children, and that they wanted to go out to protect them." White officers claimed the mayor's assurances calmed the men, but a roll call that day revealed that two hundred men were absent from the fort. Their behavior awaits detailed study of the Memphis riot. We have only the testimony of Tony Cherry, a young discharged soldier who shelled corn on the Mississippi levee and who told the congressional committee that some blacks fired at the white rioters, using "old shot guns they got out of the houses." . . .

A vast amount of other data show that Afro-Americans emerged from slavery with far more than shattered family experiences. What these data disclose about *who* the ex-slaves were in 1865 is reason to re-examine how these men and women behaved after 1865. But the same evidence does not hint at *how* and *why* their condition had come to pass. No more misleading inference could be drawn from these data than to argue that they show that slaves lived in stable families. The typical Virginia ex-slave family in 1865, for example, had two parents in it, but many of the early marriages broken by force that were reported by elderly Mississippi and northern Louisiana slaves in 1864 and 1865 had been broken years before in Upper South states like Virginia. Poor ex-slaves living in Virginia and North Carolina in 1865 had brothers and sisters as well as aunts and uncles and cousins in that year who lived in Mississippi and northern Louisiana.

Understanding how these ex-slaves in 1865 had retained a strong family identification in the Lower as well as in the Upper South requires modification of the prevalent "models" of slave socialization and behavior that characterize much of the writing of slave history. Such "models" usually greatly minimize and sometimes entirely ignore the adaptive capacities of African slaves and several generations of Afro-American slaves. How slaves learned and whom they learned from always affected what they believed and therefore how they behaved and the choices they made. External constraints affected slave behavior, too, so that slave behavior and slave belief were not always congruent. A vast and diverse scholarly literature, however, seeks to explain slave beliefs and behavior by studying little more than *what* enslavement *did to* Afro-Americans. Such study sparks frequent disputes about whether slaves were "well" or "badly" treated, a recurrent exercise in historical demonology. U. B. Phillips, the generation of historians he so profoundly influenced, and nearly all his most severe critics studied mostly what enslavement did to Afro-Americans. Their answers varied. Racists like Phillips found in bondage institutional arrangements meant to "civilize" Africans. Critics, including such able scholars as Frazier, Kenneth M. Stampp, and Stanley M. Elkins, sharply rejected the racial assumptions of Phillips and his followers but focused on the same question. A detailed and often useful monographic literature on nineteenth-century slavery, moreover, nearly always explains variations in slave behavior as responses to *external stimuli* such as location (e.g., the Upper or the Lower South), the size and function of a productive unit (e.g., a farm or plantation), and the attitudes of slaveowners (e.g., "cruel" or "humane" and "capitalist" or "paternalist"). Such differences are very important in explaining variations in slave belief and behavior, but implicit or explicit reductionist biases affect this influential conceptualization of the slave experience. Early-twentieth-century scholars nearly all believed that slaves could learn only from their owners so that slave culture, a source of slave belief and behavior, was at best "imitative." Later-twentieth-century historians and social scientists substitute behavioral "models" for this crude belief but still often contend that slave belief and behavior involved little more than responses to master-sponsored external stimuli.

How enslavement and the decisions of owners affected Africans and their Afro-American descendants needs careful study, but to examine only that is not to study Afro-American belief and behavior. Variations in owner behavior matter greatly, nearly always defining the external limits of slave behavior. But the study of slave "treatment," in itself invaluable, is not the same as the study of the development of a viable slave culture with its own standards of correct behavior, what the anthropologist Sidney W. Mintz describes as "the repertory of socially-learned and inculcated resources of the enslaved." Inadequate study of how there developed among Afro-American slaves what Mintz calls "historically-derived values, behavior patterns, and practices" obscures and even distorts the meaning of accurately observed slave behavior. A single example drawn from the 1865-1866 Virginia population censuses and marriage registers illustrates this point. This evidence shows that most Virginia slaves lived in two-parent households and that many slave marriages were long-lasting. Three questions, among others, need to be asked to assess its meaning. Are the particular data accurate? If so, why did most slaves live in such households and why did many slave marriages last so long? And finally, what do such regularities in slave behavior disclose about slave beliefs? Answers to the second and third questions cannot be inferred from observed behavior. They result, in part, from the historian's conceptualization of slave society and of the social processes that shaped everyday slave behavior. To assume that slave behavior was primarily a function of slave "treatment" promises different explanations than the assumption that slave belief had its origins within a cumulative slave experience. If most owners, for example, forced their slaves to live with spouses, the length of slave marriages and the composition of slave households would disclose nothing about slave beliefs. But if most owners did not require that slave husbands and wives remain together, the length of slave marriages is extremely important evidence about slave culture and the norms it upheld.

Yet another corrective perspective is needed so that reasons ex-slaves retained such strong family ties are properly understood. It also has to do with socialization. Most studies of slave behavior are *static* in conception and in execution. Slave behavior is examined at a particular moment in time, not over a lengthy time. That perspective makes it nearly impossible to examine how slaves responded to changes in their external circumstance and how one generation of slaves learned from slaves in earlier generations. Mintz points out that slavery "gave rise to special conditions of cultural change," compelling the slaves "to fashion new life-styles in the face of tremendous repression." Study of that process requires time perspective. The slaves and ex-slaves described in this chapter—those living in diverse Virginia, North Carolina, Mississippi, northern Louisiana, Tennessee, and Kentucky settings—were not "slaves." *They were the last generation of slaves.*

Philip D. Curtin's very important study *The Atlantic Slave Trade: A Census* (1969) reinforces the need to study slave behavior in an enlarged time perspective. Curtin estimates the number of Africans imported into the United States at slightly less than half a million. By the emancipation, the Afro-American population had increased to more than nine times the number imported, a rapid natural increase that started in the first half of the eighteenth century and continued throughout the period of enslavement. Such population growth contrasted sharply with that of other New World slave populations and, as C. Vann Woodward writes, remains "a neglected historical experience," one that "has gone virtually unnoticed or has been taken for granted by historians of the United States." Curtin's study, moreover, demonstrates that of the fewer than half million Africans brought to the North American continent, nearly half (about 46 percent) came between 1741 and 1780 and about another 25 percent between 1781 and the abolition of the legal slave trade in 1808.

A period of between eighty and one hundred twenty years separated nearly half of the enslaved Africans brought to the North American mainland from their Afro-American slave descendants at the moment of the general emancipation. Only a few slave generations connect these two moments in time. But a social process of "creolization" (the transformation of the African into the Afro-American) was already well under way by the time the federal Constitution was adopted and before the invention of the cotton gin. Culture formation among the slaves, which began before the War for Independence and well before the plantation system spread from the Upper to the Lower South, blended together African and Anglo-American cultural beliefs and social practices, mediated through the harsh institution of enslavement. Most slaves involved in the spread of the plantation system and of the developing Afro-American culture over the entire South in the six decades prior to the Civil War were the children and the grandchildren of that adaptive eighteenth-century slave culture, a culture neither African nor American but genuinely Afro-American. We have examined briefly decisions made between 1864 and 1866 by about forty thousand different adult ex-slaves, men and women who were still together in families and who registered slave marriages at the end of this process.

The choices they made between 1864 and 1866 can only be assessed by examining how an adaptive culture had developed among them and their forebears in the century and half preceding the emancipation. That is so because slave belief and behavior at the emancipation were the consequence of a recurrent interaction between accumulating slave historical experiences (culture) as transmitted over time through an adaptive slave-family and kinship system and the changing slave society in which the slaves lived. Radical external changes regularly tested the adaptive capacities of several different slave generations. There was first the adaptation associated with initial enslavement, then the adaptation associated with the spread of plantation slavery from the Upper to the Lower South (1815 to 1860), and finally the adaptation associated with the Civil War and emancipation. How the slaves dealt with these changes in external circumstance—and with other changes which they could not affect such as the development of a farm into a plantation, the sale of a child, and the death or sale of a spouse—depended at all times upon the accumulated experiences and beliefs of the slave men and women who had lived before them. . . .

Part III

The Distribution of
Culture and Power
in the Slave Community

The Preservation of
Oral Stories
in Black Culture

GLADYS-MARIE FRY

No culture can prosper if it does not control the transmission of its values. In previous essays Levine and Gutman suggested that spirituals and models of family structure carried slave culture and social values from one generation to the next. In the first selection Wood included material culture and craft skills as important elements in cultural preservation. In this essay folklorist Gladys-Marie Fry, author of *Night Riders in Black Folk History* (1975), argues that storytelling was the social and cultural cement of the slave community. Through storytelling slaves related their own history. The stories, repeated year in and year out by elders, gave slave children a common fund of tradition and folkbelief. Were the stories always the same? Is storytelling still important in the black community? Why did slaves rely on stories to inculcate values in children? What were the social dynamics of storytelling? What does the process of storytelling imply about the social structure of the slave community? Compare Fry's suggestions about the importance of the storytelling process and content with the observations by Thomas Webber in the next selection on the socialization of slave

Reprinted from Gladys-Marie Fry, *Night Riders in Black Folk History* (Knoxville: University of Tennessee Press, 1975), pp. 212-215, without notes, by permission of the author. Copyright © 1975 Gladys-Marie Fry.

children and with the analysis by John Blassingame in a later selection on the social structure of the slave community.

That slave owners knew about—and tried to prevent—clandestine meetings of the Blacks is a historical fact. Masters perceived these nocturnal gatherings as an organizing force for the slaves, a very real threat to the slave system. What the master did not understand, or perhaps even know, was that many of these secret meetings were no more than the continuation of a practice deeply rooted in the Blacks' African heritage, and in this strange land, the only way to preserve the continuity with the past that would sustain them in the future. The Blacks needed to talk to each other; quite simply, they met to tell stories. In so doing, they continued their oral tradition, now the basis of this book. A former slave recalled to this author the moving about at night from one plantation to another for storytelling sessions at designated cabins:

> They used to sit nights and tell tales. One or two of them would come to the quarters, steal there after old master and old mistress gone to bed. They would steal to the quarter and sit down and tell tales.

During slavery, these gatherings for storytelling acted as a kind of clearinghouse of news concerning family members who had been sold or who had stolen away from the plantation. Slaves learned of births, deaths, illnesses, and separations, as well as of approaching secret meetings and social events. Indeed, information concerning every facet of life, from the private world of the slave compound to the outside arena of local and national events, was verbally disseminated in the quarters. Equally important, however, was the function of these sessions in helping to preserve the slave's sense of self-identity, of knowing who he was and how he perceived his world and objectified his experiences. These slaves who risked so much to attend forbidden secret assemblies were driven by a strong need to remember the past. Moments of conversation—fleeting though they must have been at times—offered one of the few opportunities for transported Blacks to form a verbal link with a long-remembered African past.

Stories told in the slave quarters were the first link in the storytelling tradition in the newly formed Black community. In the post-Civil War period, Black descendants channeled their need to remember their own side of the slavery experience—the perspective of the victims rather than the perpetrators—into frequent storytelling sessions at predetermined sites. Sometimes the storytelling situation was occasioned by social events, such as a church revival, a housewarming, or a lull at a frolic. Indeed, any type of gathering sooner or later spontaneously turned to storytelling.

> I recollect a good many stories told by my grandparents. As a matter of fact, when I was a child, my grandparents and other relatives of mine and people from the neighborhood used to go to my grandfather's house, and they would sit and talk on Saturdays and Sundays about what slavery was like, and I would sit and listen to them.

These were frequent sessions open to a closely knit group of tellers. Within the family unit, time was often set aside nightly for reminiscences and stories. Such accounts either accompanied boring and tedious household routines or were the basis of afterwork leisure. Oral stories which provided an escape from stark reality were usually told while some form of food was being prepared, such as roasting sweet potatoes or chestnuts, pulling molasses candy, or cranking the ice-cream freezer.

Slave narratives frequently refer to the supernatural stories told by the fireside during the long winter months. The eerie light cast by burning embers, the puffs of curling smoke, and the crackling timbers provided a dramatic setting for stories about ghosts, witches, Jack o'Lantern, "the evil eye," and Raw Head and Bloody Bones. Listeners, especially those who had come from some distance, were known to have become so distressed by these stories that they refused to leave the security of the hearthside until morning. The Reverend Earl L. Harrison remembered that

> My grandfather's sons would sit up until the wee hours of the night telling these stories. And they would tell some of the awfullest, most terrible ghost stories. Of course our houses would be built up on stilts, up off the ground, where dogs slept under the house, and hogs too. We didn't have a fence at night. And there'd be cracks in the floor, like those down there, some of them bigger than that. And I've sat up many a night with my feet up on the chair like this, afraid that something would get me through those cracks. And then they would tell me to go to bed. We'd all be sitting before a fire, you know, a fireplace with logs on the fire. Just one fireplace and you had to go out in the cold room to go to bed. And I was scared to death.

Whatever the storytelling situation, it was the constant repetition of these stories, year after year, that accounts for their tenacity in the memories of many Blacks. Individual members of the Black community became known as "good talkers" and were often identified with particular repertoires of stories. As the occasion required, these stories were repeated again and again in flawless and meticulous detail. The audience, acting as an unconscious preserving force, helped to maintain some stability of texts by calling attention to such story changes as substitutions of detail and omitted passages. Borrowing and exchanging stories occurred freely, with the opening formula, "Old Man So and So used to tell the story about. . . ."

The role of children in these storytelling sessions is an aspect of folk tradition too long overlooked. Stories about the past seemed to have had a special kind of appeal for children of slave descendants, for they listened by the hour, fascinated by the history of their family. James C. Evans recalls that

> In the evenings, we'd sit around. If it was the cool part of the weather, we'd sit around the fire, and if it was the warm summer time, just sit around the yard, and there would be two hours or more of just family talk. Maybe five of us there, maybe twenty-five of us. With the senior one always being respected as the moderator, or whatever it was. And this would go on every night.

Old people, including favorite grandparents, were especially sought out by children because of their storytelling abilities. Such a person was

> Old man Ben Jeanes [who] came up in slavery, and he used to have a lot of children to be around him. He was very amusing, and he'd tell stories about white folks and how they did him, and how he outplanned them.

In public gatherings, however, children learned to sit as quietly as possible while their elders held forth. Assuming and maintaining an inconspicuous posture was essential, for there were certain types of sensitive stories which were felt by adult Blacks to be too delicate for children's ears. But older Blacks, often caught up in the atmosphere of re-created experience, simply forgot that children were present. These children, listening mesmerized to countless tellings and retellings of a remembered past, learned of the fears, the horrors, the whole of the Black slave world. They learned, too, the storytelling tradition and passed it on to their children, forging still another link in the chain of transmission between Africa, the slave situation in the New World, and the present Black experience.

The Peer Group

THOMAS L. WEBBER

Thomas Webber concentrates on the formation of community identity and values in the slave quarters, a subject he examines more fully in his book, *Deep Like the Rivers: Education in the Slave Quarter Community, 1831-1865* (1978). The socialization of slaves began in childhood, as indeed did the sense of kinship and shared experience which fused slaves together into a community. Play was a forge of culture. Games were early lessons in survival, and roaming about the country introduced slave children to a larger world than the plantation. From their common play on the plantation the slave children developed a sense of "we" which fixed their posture when they confronted "them," or the whites. What do the children's games show about the importance of religion and family among slaves? How did the young slave learn about work? How did the young slave learn what it meant to be a slave? How did the slave's experience as a child affect his life as a slave, his response to bondage, and his conception of the slave community? What does child's play show about the social structure of the community? Compare Webber's remarks on social structure and status with Blassingame's arguments in the next selection.

From the time the children of the quarters first began to crawl and toddle about, they came into contact with other slave children. As they learned to talk, walk, and take care of themselves, these occasional contacts became more frequent until much of their walking time was spent in conversing, playing, singing, fighting, and eating with their peer group companions. The nature of the educational impact which the peer group had upon its members is suggested by the large quantity of time which peer group members spent in each other's company. For six days a week the children of the quarters passed most of the time their parents were in the fields, some ten to fourteen hours a day, in close association with the other members of their peer group.

The educational role of the peer group began at play. As with most children, the play of quarter children consisted both of games improvised on the spot and those handed down, with infinite variations, from generation to generation. Davenport says that he and the other children of the quarters, when not busy with light chores such as gathering wood and sweeping the yard, "played together in the street what run de length of the quarters. Us throwed horseshoes, jumped poles, walked on stilts, and played marbles. Sometimes us made bows and arrows. Us could shoot 'em too just like little Injuns." "De best game us had was marbles," recalls Tom Hawkins of his slave days in South Carolina, "and us played wid homemade clay marbles most of the time." Sally Murphy reports that her peer group had all the fun they wanted. "Us played jump rope and swung in de grapevine swings mostly." As a child an old Fisk informant and his friends "used to play a game we called 'smut,' but we would play it with corn spots instead of cards. We played it just like you would with cards only we would have grains of corn and call them hearts and spades, and so forth, and go by the spots on the corn."

Bert Mayfield and his companions played a game called "sheep-meat," which appears to have been a version of what is now known as dodge ball. "Sheep-meat was a game played with a yarn ball and when one of the players was hit by the ball that counted him out." "Once over" was another ball game played by the quarter children. It involved throwing a ball over one of the cabins. If the ball was caught by one of the players on the other side, that player would run around to the other side of the cabin and attempt to hit one of the other team with the ball, thus knocking him out of the game. "We'd have to make a ball out of yarn and put a sock around it for cover. Six of us would stay on one side of a house and six on the other."

Hide and seek in many varieties was also popular. "When us played our hidin' game," remembers Callie Elder, "us sung somepin' lak dis:

> Mollie, Mollie Bright
> Three score and ten,
> Can I get dere by candlelight?
> Yes, if your laigs is long enough!"

Anna Parkes recounts that in playing "Old Hundred" she and her playmates "would choose one, and dat one would hide his face agin' a tree whilst he counted to a hundud. Den he would hunt for all de others. Dey done been hidin' whilst he wuz countin'. Us larned to count a-playin' 'Ole Hundud.'"

Of those games which required a group, some of the most widely played appear to have been several different ring game extrapolations played to the rhythm of a variety of tunes. "When us was chillun in de quarters we did a mighty lot of playin'," recalls Katherine Eppes. "Us useta play 'Sail away Rauley' a whole lot. Us would hol' han's an' go 'roun' in a ring, gittin' faster an' faster an' demn what fell down was outa de game." Martha Colquitt and her peer group "used to play lots, but us never did have no special name for our playin'. 'Swingin' in de corner', was when us all joined hand in a long row, and de leader would begin to run around in circles, and at de other end of the line dey would soon be runnin' so fast dey was most flyin'."

Sometimes the play of the children involved singing, story-telling, and the asking of riddles. According to William Henry Towns, "Dere was a whole lot of games an' riddles to be played dem days. . . . De riddles was like dis:

> Slick as a mole, black as a coal,
> Got a great long tail like a thunder hole. (skillet)

> Crooked as a rainbow, teeth lak a cat,
> Guess all of your life but you can't guess dat. (blackberry
> bush)

Sometimes the slave children were allowed by their parents to continue their play at night. Josephine Hamilton says that she and her friends often "played in the moonlight." Frank Gill remembers how he and the other little children "played ball, and marbles, 'specially marbles, hit was our big game. Even after night, dey had a big light out in de back yard, an' us would play." On Jane Simpson's plantation "De white folks didn't want to let de slaves have no time for deir self, so de old folks used to let us chillun run and play at night, while de folks sleep and dey watch de stars to tell about what time to call us in and put us to bed, before de white folks know we was out."

In some quarters a special brand of fireworks marked Christmas as a highpoint for the children. Pauline Grice remembers the Christmases of her childhood as a slave on a plantation near Atlanta, Georgia:

> Us have singing and 'joyment all day. Then at night, the big fire builded, and all us sot round it. There am 'bout hundred hog bladders save from hog killing. So, on Christmas night, the children takes them and puts them on the stick. First they is blowed full of air and tied tight and dry. Then the children holds the bladder in the fire and pretty soon, "BANG!" they goes. That am the fireworks.

Often games played by quarter children were highly suggestive of situations similar to those experienced by slaves. While visiting one of her father's large cotton plantations Mary Banks encountered a group of slave children playing a game in which a circle was formed about one child in the middle who tries to break out while all sing:

> Oh, do let me out! I'z in dis lady's gyarden,
> Oh, do let me out! I'z in dis lady's gyarden.
>
> De gate iz lockt, an' de wall iz high,
> Roun' dis lady's gyarden. Chorus.
>
> De gate iz lockt, an' de key iz lo',
> Un dis lady's gyarden. Chorus.
>
> I mus', I will, git out er here,
> Out er dis lady's gyarden. Chorus.
>
> I'll break my neck but I'll get out er here,
> Out er dis lady's gyarden. Chorus.

While the singing continued, they danced around keeping time to the music, the imprisoned one making efforts all the while to escape, by trying to creep under, jump over, or break down, the wall of the lady's garden.

Finally, effecting her escape, they all attempt to elude her grasp, as the one caught takes her place in the "gyarden" and the play is thus continued, mid the shouts and laughter from all.

A former slave from Arkansas recalls a game which must have hit even closer to home called "Chick-Chick":

You'd ketch 'hold a hands and ring up. Had one outside was the hawk and some inside was the hen and chickens. The old mother hen would say—

'Chick-a-ma, chick-a-ma, craney crow, Went to the well to wash my toe; When I come back my chicken was gone, What time is it, old witch?'

One chicken was s'posed to get out and then the hawk would try to ketch him.

Two games which appeared frequently in the narratives were probably means through which slave children helped themselves to cope with two of their greatest fears—whippings and evil spirits. "Hide the Switch," in which a switch was hidden and the child who found it ran after the others in an attempt to strike them, was but one of the many forms of a game which involved slave children whipping each other. Versions of "No Bogey-man Tonight," in which one slave child pretended to be an evil spirit or the Devil and attempted to catch the others, appeared throughout the quarters of the slaveholding South.

The older children were often allowed to roam about within the confines of their home plantation, and the fields, forests, and streams provided them with hours of fun and adventure. A former slave interviewed by the Fisk project remembers that as a slave child his peer group's "biggest amusement was running through the woods, climbing trees, hunting grapes and berries and so forth." Robert Shepherd and his companions used to take to the woods in order to escape the tasks assigned by Aunt Viney, their nursery guardian. "Dere was a big sand bar down in de crick what made a fine place to play, and wadin' in de branches was lots of fun. Us frolicked up and down dem woods and had all sorts of good times—anything to keep away from Aunt Viney 'cause she was sho' to have us fetchin' in wood or sweepin' de yards if us was handy whar she could find us."

As a child Acie Thomas spent much of his time "roaming over the broad acres" of his master's Florida plantation. He and his friends "waded in the streams, fished, chased rabbits and always knew where the choicest wild berries and nuts grew." In addition to small game, berries, and nuts, the woods also produced eggs, which could be traded to the plantation cook or to the white mistress for a sweet. Julia Cole recalls that she and her friends "loved to hunt for turkey nests 'cause dey give us a teacake for evvy turkey egg us fotched in." Besides playing marbles, cat ball, base, blindfold and tag, George Rogers and the other children of his North Carolina quarters "fished a lot in Briar Creek. We caught a lot of fish. Sometimes we used pin hooks we made ourselves. We would trade our fish to missus for molasses to make candy of." Tom Hawkins and his friends used to "catch a heap of fish wid hook and line. De river and crick hole run thoo' Miss Annie's plantation so us didn't have to ax for a pass evvy time us went a fishin'."

After his master moved his slaves from Virginia to Missouri, H. C. Bruce recalls living on a large farm of about thirty-five slaves.

> I was too young to be put to work, and there being on the farm four or five boys about my age, spent my time with them hunting and fishing. There was a creek near by in which we caught plenty of fish. We made lines of hemp grown on the farm and hooks of bent pins. When we got a bite, up went the pole and quite often the fish, eight or ten feet in the air. We never waited for what is called a good bite, for if we did the fish would get the bait and escape capture, or get off when hooked if not thrown quickly upon the land. But fish then were very plentiful and not as scary as now. The hardest job with us was digging bait. We often brought home as much as five pounds of fish in a day.

Sometimes slaves took the opportunity of their childhood leisure to acquaint themselves with the children of neighboring quarter communities. "The patteroles never bothered the children any," reports Allen Johnson. "The children couldn't go anywhere without the consent of the mother and father. And there wasn't any danger of them running off. If they caught a little child between plantations, they would probably just run them home. It was all right for a child to go in the different quarters and play with one another during daytime just so they got back before night." Silas Jackson, who grew up on a plantation of over one hundred slaves near Ashbie Gap, Virginia, says,"We boys used to take the horns of a dead cow or bull, cut the end off of it, we could blow it, some having different notes. We could tell who was blowing and from what plantation."

Association with peer group members also allowed the children of the quarters to practice roles which they would assume more fully later in life. A favorite pastime, for instance, was "playing grown-ups." Dolls were made with old rags and doll houses (sometimes elaborate play houses) were made with wood, bark, stones, and leaves. The girls would dress up in their mothers' handkerchiefs and aprons and would make necklaces from corn beads and earrings from peanuts split opened at one end. Besides hunting and fishing, the boys refined their singing and storytelling abilities, and practiced their whittling and basket weaving skills.

Both boys and girls played at conjuration and religion. One informant in the Federal Writers' Project study recalls that on his plantation he and the other children "used to play preachin' and baptisin'. We'd put 'em down in the water and souse 'em and we'd shout just like the old folks." Benny Dilliard recalls his life as a slave in Georgia:

Us would play make-believe preachin' and baptizin' and de way us would sing was a sight. One of dem songs us children loved de best went lak dis:

"Why does you thirst
By de livin' stream?
And den pine away
And den go to die.

Why does you search
For all dese earthy things?
When you all can
Drink at de livin' spring,
And den can live."

When us started playin' lak us was baptizin' 'em, us th'owed all us could ketch right in de crick, clothes and all, and ducked 'em. Whilst us was singin':

"Git on board, git on board
For de land of many mansions,

Same old train dat carried
My Mammy to de Promised Land."

Within the peer group most slave children began to experiment with their courting techniques and to experience their first post-pubescent sexual encounters. Henry Lewis remembers clearly the "well-game" played among the boys and girls of his peer group. "De gal or boy set in de chair and lean way back and pretend like dey in de well. Dey say so many feet down and say, 'Who you want pull you out?' And de one you want pull you out, dey s'posed to kiss you." Lucindy Johnson recounts that when she and her girl friends went courting "us went to walk an' hunted chestnuts. Us would string dem an' put 'em 'round our necks an' smile at our fellers."

When nothing more exciting occurred to them, the children would watch the old folks at work. As a child Randel Lee "delighted in stopping around the tanning yard and watching the men salt the hide."

It was often in the company of peer group members that the children of the quarters had their first experiences in dealing with whites. Henry Watson recalls how, upon the arrival of a strange white, he and the other slave children would run "and hide ourselves until the man had gone." Other former slaves recall how they were spanked with their heads between their masters' knees or forced to sing and dance for master and his company. Others remember how in the company of their peer group members they first heard the tenets of slaveholding priestcraft. It was also in the peer group, given courage by the company of their friends, that children first began to steal eggs, tobacco, and other desired goods. "Us children," confesses Tom Hawkins, "used to tie up de 'bacco, what us stole f'um Miss Annie, in de under-arm part of de long sleeves of our shirts." David Gullins tells how he and his associates learned together as children to outwit their mistress:

> Some days Mistress was good and kind to us little niggers, and she would save us the cold biscuits to give to us when we brought in the eggs. Sometimes, she would go two or three days without giving us any biscuits then she didn't get no eggs. We rascals would get up the eggs and go off and have a rock battle with them. Every effect has a cause—then Miss would wonder why she didn't get any eggs and call us all in for cold biscuits, then the eggs would come again. Of course we had our game of "tell." If one of the gang threatened to tell, then we all would threaten to tell all we knew on him, and somehow we managed to get by with it all.

Sometimes peer group members were able to acquire a skill which they could share with each other. Whether the teaching was deliberate or not, peer group members learned from each other how to sing, dance, whittle, hunt, play musical instruments, and sometimes, even, read. Acie Thomas claims to have known "all the wood lore common to children of his time. This he learned mostly from 'cousin Ed' who was several years older than he and quite willing to enlighten a small boy in these matters." Sam Aleckson had two special friends, Joe and Hector. "These boys were somewhat older than myself. They were skilled in woodcraft, and taught me how to make bird traps and soon had me out hunting."

As they grew older and reached the time when they were forced to join the plantation work force, it was with peer group brothers and sisters that slave children first discovered the reality of their slave status and began to discuss among themselves what it meant to live under slavery. The shock of ending what for many had been a relatively carefree childhood and beginning field work in earnest was eased by the continued companionship of the peer group. Though their leisure time was now drastically curtailed, even in the fields they could talk, sing, and help each other bear the burdens of slavery.

This is not to say that all the children of a given quarter community necessarily thought of each other as brothers and sisters, but to suggest that each child had his or her own special friend, or group of friends, who became an extension of that child's family and played an important role in his education. Though unrelated by blood, peer brothers and sisters often shared a common grandparent. A child whose father was absent often adopted the father of a peer brother as his role model. And, whatever the outlook of the adult world around them, the children of the quarters made no distinction between "biological" and "peer" and often took more seriously their felt and assumed responsibility to peer brothers and sisters than that felt for actual siblings. Campbell and two of his friends agreed to help each other even to the point of stopping the overseer from whipping any one of them. When Isaac Mason attempted to escape with two other slaves, they "knelt down and prayed and then took an oath that we would fight for each other till we died."

Sometimes the peer group was even forced to assume almost all of the functions of the family. George Kye, who was born on a large farm in Arkansas, did not sleep at his mother's cabin and was unsure whether or not he had any blood-line brothers or sisters. "My mammy was named Jenny and I don't think I had any brothers or sisters, but they was a whole lot of children at the quarters that I played with. I didn't live with Mammy because she worked all the time, and us children all stayed in one house. It was a little one room log cabin, chinked and daubed, and you couldn't stir us with a stick."

In most quarter communities there was only one group of children of approximately the same age. Thus, although the slave child could choose, theoretically, to remain aloof from her peer group, she could not choose from among different groups. The children of the quarters could no more choose with whom they wished to associate than they could choose their biological parents. The slave child either ran with the other children of her age group or she ran with no one. For most children no such conscious choice ever occurred to them. The bonds of love and mutual need formed between peer group members were molded too early and too strongly to ever suggest themselves to the slave child as anything else than the way things naturally were. The important role which peer group brothers and sisters played in each others' lives well into the adulthood is described in the following passage by Frederick Douglass:

> For much of the happiness, or absence of misery, with which I passed this year, I am indebted to the genial temper and ardent friendship of my brother slaves. They were every one of them manly, generous, and brave. Yes, I say they were brave, and I will add, fine-looking. It is seldom the lot of any one to have truer friends than were the slaves of their farm. It was not uncommon to charge slaves with treachery towards each other, but I must say that I never loved, esteemed, or confided in men more than I did these. They were as true as steel, and no band of brothers could be more loving. There were no mean advantages taken of each other, no tattling, no giving each other bad names to Mr. Freedland, and no elevating one at the expense of the others. We never undertook anything of any importance which was likely to affect each other without mutual consultation. We were generally a unit, and moved together. Thoughts and sentiments were exchanged between us which might well have been considered incendiary had they been known by our masters.

As slaves grew old enough to work, to marry, and to raise a family of their own, the amount of time which they were able to spend with other peer group members diminished. The roles, friendships, values, attitudes, and understandings formed within the peer group, however, continued, and served as an important foundation upon which slaves acted as adult members of the quarter community.

Status and Social Structure
in the
Slave Community

JOHN W. BLASSINGAME

With his valuable study, *The Slave Community: Plantation Life in the Antebellum South* (1972), John Blassingame made one of the most telling, sustained assaults on Stanley Elkins' Sambo thesis. Relying principally on slave autobiographies, Blassingame portrayed the slaves as creative, African-rooted, adaptive people—anything but the infantile, passive creatures Elkins described. Blassingame continues his search for the real slave in this essay on status and social structure among slaves. He rejects the traditional association between a slave's occupation and his place in the plantation pecking order, for it implies that the master's values and interests were accepted by the slaves. Using the slaves' oral tradition, Blassingame reorders the slaves' social structure, for he finds that the slaves accorded the highest status to those slaves who were the farthest removed from the master's interest and who resisted the master. Slaves admired religious leaders, good storytellers, craftsmen, singers and musicians, and teachers. Elders especially enjoyed deference and respect among the slaves. What common attributes did all these respected slaves share? In what ways did the social structure of the slave community reflect the prevalence of Afro-

Acknowledgment to the University Press of Mississippi for permission to reprint "Status and Social Structure in the Slave Community: Evidence from New Sources" by John W. Blassingame, from *Perspectives and Irony in American Slavery,* edited by Harry P. Owens. Copyright © 1976 University Press of Mississippi.

American culture among the slaves? What does the distribution of status show about slave values? In what ways did the master's influence intrude to order the structure of the slave community? What are Blassingame's assumptions about the coherence of the slave community? Compare Blassingame's emphasis on slave resistance with the suggestions of Genovese in a previous essay and with the remarks of Charles Joyner in the next selection. Are culture and society the same?

The great scholar J. Winston Coleman in his study, *Slavery Times in Kentucky*, described many of the elements of status in the quarters accepted by historians. According to Coleman, the house servant was "one of the most desirable positions on the whole plantation. The house servants formed a class quite distinct from, and socially above, the field hands; in fact . . . they assumed an air of superiority over the field hands and sometimes refused to recognize them. . . . Also, slaves often rated their social standing by their value in the market." A number of historians added the mulatto, the driver, and the artisan to those accorded high status in the quarters. While Coleman typifies the traditional view, Kenneth Stampp has been the historian most sensitive to the true nature of slave social structure. Yet, he too contended in *The Peculiar Institution* that "domestics, artisans, and foremen constituted the aristocracy of slave society." In *The Slave Community* I agreed with the theory when I wrote: "those slaves who held some important post in the plantation hierarchy were ascribed higher status in the quarters than the mass of slaves."

This view of slave social structure is much too simplistic. The house servant, driver, mulatto, and artisan have been mistakenly placed at the top of the slave hierarchy because historians unwittingly assumed that a bondsman's status depended on two things— how much personal contact he had with the planter and how valuable his services were to the master. Since it enhanced the planter's ego to view a slave's status in this way, the plantation records usually relied upon by scholars are misleading when considering slave social structure.

Two steps must be taken in order for scholars to develop new ways of looking at slave social structure. First, of course, is more systematic exploration of sociological theory. Second, new sources

on slave life must be examined. In preparing this study, I initially
reviewed the black folklore collected by J. Mason Brewer, A. M.
Christensen, Alan Dundes, and Elsie Clews Parsons. Then I turned
to the Works Progress Administration era interviews recently compiled by George Rawick. I have, however, restricted my purview
to that of the most reliable volume in the collection, Fisk University's *Unwritten History of Slavery*. Finally, I have used material
from my own collection of slave letters, speeches, interviews, and
autobiographies written between 1736 and 1938. What do these
sources reveal about the accuracy of our traditional view of the
roots of status in the slave community? How true, for example, is
the proposition that light skin color played a significant role in
status groupings in the quarters?

The slaves interviewed by Fisk University in 1929 refer so
frequently to mulattoes as "yellow bitches" and the sons thereof
that it is difficult to accept the proposition that simply being nearly
white was any guarantee of status. On the contrary, it was a mark
of degradation. Indeed, mulatto slaves expressed such hatred for
their white fathers that light skin color was clearly as much of a
liability as an advantage in the quarters. An Alabama bondswoman
recalled that, although mulatto slaves thought they were better
than blacks, she felt the "Lamp Black" slave was "de mos' 'penda-
ble cau'se he is 'honest got.'" Others have made similar arguments.
In an 1842 speech the Kentucky bondsman Lewis Clarke asserted,
"The slaves used to debate together sometimes, what could be the
reason the yellow folks couldn't be trusted like the dark ones
could. As a general rule, they seemed to be dissipated, devil-may-
care fellows; and I'll tell you what we concluded was the reason—
we concluded it was because they was sons of their masters, and
took after their fathers. . . . I have heard 'em talk on about it, . . .
till I felt ashamed of the white blood that was in me."

Since practically all slaves distrusted house servants, it is illogi-
cal to assume that at the same time they accorded them great
status. The degree of personal contact a slave had with whites was
inversely related to his or her status in the quarters. A Tennessee
house servant interviewed in 1929 observed that the other slaves
"wouldn't say anything before me, 'cause I stayed in the house,
and et in there, and slept in there." While it may have been attractive because of better and more food and clothing, the position of
house servant was rejected by all blacks who had not been trained
for it since childhood. The house servant was taught by the planter
that he was superior to other blacks. The house servants included
in the *Unwritten History of Slavery* constantly reiterated this

point. "Mistress," one of them noted, "used to tell me not to play with the colored children so much 'cause I wasn't like they was." If the slave had grown up in the master's household, he often accepted such views. But many others saw that, inasmuch as they were socially confined and constantly under the surveillance of whites, they had the least desirable job on the plantation.

In addition to being forced to look upon a sea of white faces, the house servant, when compared to the field slave, led a sterile life. A former Mississippi slave declared: "I liked the field work better than I did the house work. We could talk and do anything we wanted to, just so we picked cotton: we used to sing and have lots of fun." Kenneth Stampp expressed the same idea in a different way when he noted that for the slave, "Living intimately with even a paternal master was not in all respects as completely satisfying as the whites liked to think." If historians move beyond the literal acceptance of the self-serving testimony of house servants and their masters, they may find the position of house servant at the very bottom of the slave's social ladder. House servants who achieved high standing among blacks did so in spite of their positions. Many of them had so many relatives and friends among the field hands that they could never identify totally with the master's interest. Consequently, when house servants were able to walk that thin line between maintaining the *appearance* of loyalty to masters with the *reality* of serving their fellow blacks, they ranked high as *individuals* in the black hierarchy.

From a psychological vantage point, as Eugene Genovese has pointed out, the driver was in an ambivalent position. That the slaves clearly understood this is revealed in the old Jamaican proverb "The driver flogs his own wife first." Still, the driver was usually too close to the master. Like the overseer, it was a hated position. Socially the driver was near the bottom of the slave hierachy. An individual driver could move out of the depths only if he were skillful enough to protect the slaves.

The contentions of J. Winston Coleman notwithstanding, the price paid for a slave had little impact on his status. It is significant, for example, that rarely did any of the slaves in the Fisk compilation mention their sale price. Since being sold was such a painful and humiliating experience for slaves, few of them could take *any* pride in *any* aspect of the transaction. A Mississippi slave remembered her sale at age eleven with loathing: "They 'xamine you just like they do a horse; they look at your teeth, and pull your eyelids back and look at your eyes, and you feel just like you was a horse." She did not mention how much her new master paid for her. The blacks included in my research reacted the same way. The Reverend John Sella Martin wrote that on the occasion of his first sale it was difficult "to describe my despair or to make known my sense of humiliation at being put upon the auction block." The second time, when he was sold for $1700, Martin observed that he "ascended the auction-block—shall I say with shame? Yes: but this second time that I adorned this hideous medium of exchange I fear there was some hate mingled with my humiliation." In 1853, former Kentucky slave Lewis Hayden described the time when his master "sold all my brothers and sisters at auction. I stood by and saw them sold. When I was just going upon the block, he swapped me off for a pair of carriage-horses. I looked at those horses with strange feelings. . . . How I looked at those horses, and walked around them, and thought for *them* I was sold."

Many slaves thought it best not to talk about their sale price, because masters often equated how much labor blacks should perform with how much they had paid for them. Reflecting on this propensity of the plantation owners, a slave said that at her sale: "When my marster bought me he paid a heap o' money for me, eighteen hundred dollars. 'If you don' make dat money good what I pay for yer,' he said, 'you know what I do ter yer.' "

If the traditional view is incorrect, then what were the actual bases for status in the quarters? Although Professor Stampp discussed many of them in 1956, no historian has yet utilized his observations in any systematic attempt to analyze black social structure. Stampp stressed the loyalty of slaves to each other, their own internal class structure, and wrote that whatever masters did, "the stratification of slave society also resulted from an impelling force within the slaves themselves . . . the white caste's whole way of life was normally far beyond the reach of slaves. In slave society, therefore, success, respectability, and morality were measured by other standards, and prestige was won in other ways." While I rejected Stampp's contention that the slaves' search for prestige was "pathetic," or that "the unlettered slaves rarely won distinction or found pleasure in intellectual or esthetic pursuits," his emphasis on the internal bases for status is correct. Analyses of social structure will never advance until this fact is accepted and a distinction is made between the roots of a slave's self-esteem and the basis of his status. There is, for instance, little light shed on social structure by Stampp's assertion that slave artisans and domestic servants obtained "a pleasant feeling of self-importance" from jobs well done.

However much personal gratification a bondsman obtained

from a job, occupations translated into high social standing in the slave community only if they combined some of the following features: (1) mobility, which allowed the slave to leave the plantation frequently, (2) freedom from constant supervision by whites, (3) opportunity to earn money and (4) provision of a direct service to other blacks. Blacks who worked as drivers, teamsters, riverboatmen, carpenters, jockeys, blacksmiths, millwrights, shoemakers, seamstresses, distillers, and any slave who hired his own time gained status among other blacks because their jobs had one or more of these features. Occupation alone earned no one the top rung of the slave social ladder.

Despite all that historians have written in the past, slaves reserved the top rungs of the social ladder for those blacks who performed services for other slaves rather than for whites. However, slave social structure was so complex and so fluid, and the sources so misleading, that it is difficult to determine exactly who the social leaders were. Consider, for instance, the black preacher. Many historians have unthinkingly assigned the minister the highest social standing because religion seemed so crucial in all of the slave sources that have survived. The place of religion in slave life has been distorted, because most of the slave witnesses who recorded their stories of bondage were relatively old. Since the church has always been the refuge of the old, they may have overemphasized the importance of religion in their lives. With this *caveat* in mind, it is possible to examine dispassionately the relationship between service and status in the slave community.

At the top of the slave social ladder the conjuror and the preacher struggled for primacy. More often than not, the conjuror won. Claiming to have received his power from God, but believed by many to be in league with the devil, the conjuror was respected, feared, and appealed to by saints and sinners alike. Although many of the church-going blacks who talked to the white WPA interviewers in the 1930s disclaimed any belief in conjurors, they consistently said the opposite in the latter half of the nineteenth century. The former slaves interviewed between 1872 and 1900 reported an almost universal faith in the conjuror; he played a prominent role in black folk tales and received more deference than any other figure in the antebellum South. Generally, slaves bowed when they met him. A former slave reminiscing about the antebellum conjuror in the 1890s asserted that the slaves "worshipped him as if he were a priest."

Since the primary concern of all people in the nineteenth century was the maintenance of good health, the black physicians were near the top of the slave social structure. Midwives and those blacks with the greatest knowledge of the medicinal value of herbs and roots performed an important service in the quarters. One indication of their status was the constant complaint of southern whites that slaves consistently preferred to follow the advice of black root doctors rather than white physicians. The bondsman's concern over his health was, of course, one of the bases for the high social standing of the conjuror.

One of the most important ways for a slave to gain status was to be skilled in what folklorists call the verbal arts. The best practitioners of the verbal arts, according to one slave, were recognized as entertainers. He recalled in 1899 that a typical plantation party "would start off with a general greeting and conversation. Telling tales ... was a common mode of entertaining. Next would come the guessing of riddles propounded by the more erudite portion of the company." Unfortunately, the party tales and riddles contained such explicit references to sex that the collectors either never heard or refused to print the more salacious ones.

Regardless of the stress laid on religion by old former slaves, the thoughts and actions of young plantation blacks, like most other youths, centered on sex, courtship, and marriage. To achieve any success in these areas, the slave had to be skilled in the verbal arts. Fortunately for the historian, nineteenth-century folklorists were keenly interested in slave courtship patterns. Courtship on the plantation was a battle of wits played by resort to riddles, poetic boasting, toasts, and ridicule. Older slaves taught the young the complicated formulas. As Frank Banks recalled,

> Among the slaves there were regular forms of "courtship," and almost every large plantation had an experienced old slave who instructed young gallants in the way in which they should go in the delicate matter of winning the girls of their choice. ... "Uncle Gilbert" [the teacher on his plantation] held the very generally accepted opinion that "courtin' is a mighty ticklish bizness" and that he who would "git a gal wuth havin, mus' know how to talk fur her."

A few examples may illustrate the courtship formula. First, of course, a man had to find out if a woman was eligible by asking, "Kin' lady, since I have been trav'lin up hill, vally an mountain, I nebber seed a lady dat suit my fancy mo' so den you does. Now is you a towel dat had been spun, or a towel dat had been woven? (Answer—if spun, single.)" Or he might say, "Are you a rag on the bush or a rag off the bush? (Answer—If a rag on the bush, free, if off, engaged.)"

Secondly, the slave seeking a partner had to ascertain whether he was an acceptable suitor. He would ask, "My dear kin' miss, has you any objections to me drawing my cher to yer side, and revolvin' de wheel of my conversation around de axle of your understandin'?" To demonstrate her acceptance of a suitor, the slave girl had to make a clever response to such questions. She might respond by saying: "I hears dat you is a dove flyin' from lim' to lim' wid no where to res' your weary wings. I's in de same condition an' hopes you kin fin' a place to res' you' heart." When accepted as a suitor, the slave then proceeded by a series of toasts and poetic allusions to convert the one of his choice:

> Dear me, kin' Miss, you is de damsel of my eye,
> Where my whole joy and pleasure lie,
> If I has some money I'll give you a part
> If I has no money I'll give you my heart.

Once a successful courtship ended, there was a distinction made between couples on the basis of the way they were united. A "proper wedding," with a black or white minister officiating, was held in high esteem. A Missouri slave, Jennie Hill, said, "In the south . . . when a couple marries they just start living together without any ceremony. . . . But I was really married, My husband and I went to a slave on his place who could read and write and knew something of the Bible. . . . I was proud of my marriage . . . and I sure got mad when anybody said anything about us not being married."

Older slaves often demonstrated their verbal skills at church. Historians, folklorists, and novelists have often described the linguistic skills of the antebellum preacher. Few of them, however, have looked at the other members of the congregation. One of the primary marks of a slave's piety was his or her ability to bear public witness to God in the form of prayer. The person most adept at this, at making the congregation feel good, was always called upon to lead in prayer. In 1897, a former slave asserted, with some exaggeration, that during the antebellum period, "All that was required to make one good was to be able to pray a prayer or be a good singer." Religious testimony was so important that slaves reduced prayers to formulas and taught them to young converts. Intoned in a rhythmical melodious chant, these prayers employed fervid imagery and an impressive succession of metaphors and vivid pictures with pauses for audience response. A former slave remembered that at the night meetings on his plantation, a bondsman would offer the following prayer:

O! Lord here it is again and again and one time more that we thine
weak an' unprofitable servants has permitted to bow, and I ask you
while I make this feeble attempt to bow that you would bow my head
below my knees, and my knees away down in some lonesome valley of
humility where you have promised to hear and answer prayer at every
time of need and every stressful hour for Jesus sake. *(Moan)*

We believe that love is growing old and sin is growing bold and Zion
wheel is clogged and can't roll, neither can she put on her beautiful
garments, but we ask you to come this way, seal her with love, type her
with blood and send her around the hill sides clucking to her broods
and bringing live sons and daughters to the marvelous light of thy glorious gospel as the bees to the honey comb and the little doves to the
windows of Noah's ark, I pray thee. *(Moan)* . . . when I come down to
death please rise our blood-bought spirits high and happy and our
bodies be lowed to our mother dust for Christ sake. A-men. *(Long
moans)*

The elite slaves in the quarters were the best singers and the
creators of black music. Songs were such a crucial accompaniment
of plantation labor, rowing boats, and husking corn, that a good
singer might receive extra perquisites from his master. A writer in
1895 contended that "the singing of the slaves at work was regarded by their masters as almost indispensable to the quick and
proper, performance of the labor, . . . that the leaders of the
singing were often excused from work that they might better attend
to their part of the business." Whether they sang spirituals, work
songs, or dance songs, the singers joined those blacks most adept
at playing musical instruments among the most respected entertainers in the quarters. Singers and musicians performed an important service in the slave community by providing solace to those
wearied in mind and body.

Another group of creators also achieved status. They were
the slaves who left their mark on the material culture—the slave
woman who became a skilled seamstress and made beautiful quilts;
the old man who could carve exquisite walking canes or whistles
for youngsters; the bondsmen who made beautiful chairs, tables,
beds, brooms, straw hats, and baskets; the woman who knew just
the plants to use in dying cloth to make colorful clothes; the man
who could make the best traps and seines; the women or men who
were noted for their ability to prepare the most succulent rabbit,
oppossum, raccoon, fish, barbecue, ginger cake, or molasses candy;
and the person making the most potent wine, persimmon beer,
cider, or whiskey. All stood high on the slave social ladder.

Nativity was one of the keys to status in the quarters. Every slave thought that work was lighter, masters kinder, and life better for blacks in his state than in any other. The former Louisiana bondsman, Alexander Kenner, testified in 1863, "The negroes in Mississippi are more stupid than those in Louisiana, on account of the masters being more cruel and oppressive." A Maryland slave's view was even more localized. Reporting that he had been to Virginia a few times, in 1863 he observed, "Slavery is harder down there than in Maryland. They have larger plantations and more servants, and they seem to be more severe. Down in Prince George's County, Md., they are a littler harder than they are in the upper part of the State." Slaves in the state, county or on the plantation generally ranked above those born outside these confines. The exception to the rule was native-born Africans who were revered by practically all blacks.

Cunning was another highly valued trait in the quarters. The bondsman who was a good hustler, cool cat, and confidence man in his effort to steal food for himself and others or who taught slaves how to avoid labor while appearing to work hard was held in high esteem in the slave community. In avoiding the lash, for example, youngsters learned from the cool cats that the way to make their quota of cotton was to pick as much as possible when the dew was still on it, to urinate on it, or to add rocks or watermelons to your pile and remove them before the cotton was ginned. The cool cat was the most frequent character in the slave folk tales. A consummate liar, a master at deceit, the cool cat was admired primarily because he was able to fool whites. Many of the jokes slaves told about themselves centered on the cool cat. He appears, for instance, in the story of the "Hog Thief":

Once an old slave used to make it his practice to steal hogs. The way he would be sure of the animal was he would tie one end of a rope around his prey and the other around himself. The old Negro had been successful for many years in his occupation, but one time when he caught one of his master's hogs he met his equal in strength. He was fixing to have a big time on the next day, which was Sunday. He was thinking about it and had the old hog going along nicely, but at last as he was coming up on the top of a very high hill the hog got unmanageable and broke loose from the old fellow's arms. Still the old man made sure it was all right because of the rope which tied them together, so he puffed and pulled and scuffed, till the hog got the best of him and started him to going down the steep hill. The hog carried him clear to his master's house, and the master and his family were sitting on the porch. All the Negro could say, as the hog carried him around and around the house by his master, was "Master, I come to bring your pig home!"

Teachers were highly esteemed in the quarters. Old men and women with great stores of riddles, proverbs, and folktales played a crucial role in teaching morality and training the youth to solve problems and to develop their memories. These cultural forms were all the more important because many of them came directly from Africa. Told by African-born slaves to their grandchildren, the ancient lore retained many of the motifs, structures, elaborate innuendoes, and much of the figurative speech characteristic of the originals. Probably about half of the lore was born out of the crucible of slavery and can be attributed to unknown individual creators. The riddle and the tale were the most important educational tools. Since a youngster's status among his peers was partially dependent on how accurately he recounted a tale or riddle he had heard from his elders, he early learned the importance of memorizing details. This early memory training is, I believe, the key to the remarkable accuracy of the memoirs of illiterate blacks so characteristic of the slave interviews and narratives and recently illustrated anew by Nate Shaw in *All Go 's Dangers*.

Since propounding and solving riddles involved both reasoning from the known to the unknown and answering deep philosophical questions, this practice was the central factor in the slave's development of analytical skills. Anyone examining slave riddles will find it easier to understand the seemingly amazing philosophical bent and impressive analyses of a William Wells Brown, Frederick Douglass, or Nate Shaw.

Literate slaves had even more status than those who taught by resort to proverb, tale, and riddle, because they could read the Bible, tell the bondsmen what was transpiring in the newspapers, and write letters and passes. Many slaves and former bondsmen have discussed the status of the literate slave in the quarters. A fugitive slave in Canada declared in 1863 that among the slaves there were some "who can read and write some, and of course their influence will bear upon the others." One of these literate bondsmen, John Sella Martin, reported that his ability to read books and newspapers to Georgia slaves "elevated me to the judgment seat of a second young Daniel among them."

Among the slaves accorded the highest status in the quarters was the rebel, i. e., the bondsman who resisted floggings, violated the racial taboos, or who ran away from the plantation. Described as "high blooded" or "bad niggers" by their admirers, these bondsmen found a central place in slave lore and songs. One indication of the rebel's status was that antebellum blacks often dated important events in their lives in relationship to Nat Turner's insurrection. Almost universally, fugitive slaves found aid in the quarters. The blacks spoke with pride of slaves who were so intractable that they frightened whites. An Alabama bondswoman reported, "Dere wuz lot'ta mean' niggers' in dem days too. Some 'Niggers' so mean dat white fo'ks didn't bodder 'em much. Ever'body knowed dey wuz mean. Will Marks wuz a bad 'Nigger' . . . . White fo'ks jes' scaid o' him . . . . Ma' marster use'ta talk 'bout killin' im an' Miss Ann tell'im 'You bedder not put your hands on dat 'Nigger,' he kill ya.' "

There were a number of general things which contributed to slave status. These included the possession of attractive clothes, skill in making garden plots bloom, physical strength, ability to read signs about the weather and to interpret dreams, and providing adequately for one's family. Age graduations represent one of the keys to social structure with elders being viewed as the possessors of wisdom, the closest link to the African homeland, and persons to be treated with respect. A slave child who insulted an old person was usually punished by that person and then later punished by his parents.

If, as scholars recognize in studying all other groups, slaves themselves ranked their fellows, we must discard the traditional characterization of slave social structure in favor of an in-group derived schema. The tentative suggestions made above represent one alternative way of viewing status in the quarters. Slave social structure was the most fluid in antebellum America. Since a slave had a 50/50 chance of being sold by the time he or she was fifty years old, the membership of every associational group changed constantly. A Protestant slave who enjoyed great status in the Upper South for piety might lose it forever, for instance, by being sold to Catholic Louisiana. Being under the control of the master, the slave's occupation often changed quickly. Besides this, most slaves were jacks-of-all-trades with "servants" and "artisans" often doing field labor. It was the rare large plantation where the division of labor was so rigid that a slave man or woman spent a lifetime working at one job. Or, as the slaves expressed it in one of their proverbs: "Tomorrow may be the carriage driver's day for plowing." Assuming that most of the observations made above are correct, the slave's valuation of roles can be represented by dividing the bondsmen into three classes:

A. Upper Class
1. Conjurors
2. Physicians and midwives

3. Preachers
4. Elders
5. Teachers
6. Creators and carriers of culture
7. Entertainers
8. Rebels

B. Middle Class
1. Creators of material culture
2. Verbal artists
3. Cool cats
4. Self-employed slaves
5. Bondsmen whose jobs frequently carried them away from the plantation
6. Artisans who made the slave's shoes, liquor, clothes and houses
7. Artisans who made the slave's tools (blacksmiths, coopers)
8. Unusually strong, handsome, pretty, or intelligent field hands
9. Drivers who protected the slave's interests

C. Lower Class
1. Temporary house servants and servants residing in the quarters
2. Ordinary field hands
3. Exploitive drivers
4. Live-in house servants with long tenure
5. Voluntary concubines
6. Informants

This model varied, of course, from one plantation to another. It has little applicability to urban slaves. The rankings, after the small elite, are least precise within classes. But whatever its short-comings, the model stresses the internal nature of the slave's so-cial structure. When viewed in this way it is obvious that occupation represented only one among a multitude of status-creating factors. Only when a slave identified completely with his master's interest did he rank his fellows primarily on where they fitted into the plan-tation's occupational hierarchy. Like most other oppressed men and women, slaves did not depend solely for their prestige and status on the limited number of jobs open to them. If the slave could have aspired to the same range of jobs open to his master, then he might have placed as much stress on the prestige of occupations as did his white oppressors. The differences in the social structure of the oppressed and the oppressors continued into the twentieth century. And American blacks will continue to have a different social structure as long as they are an oppressed minority denied access to the places of power and prestige normally open to whites.

The Creolization
of
Slave Folklife

CHARLES W. JOYNER

In this final essay anthropologist and historian Charles Joyner sums up the debates on African carryovers and Afro-American culture. He scores most scholars for adopting static, one-dimensional views of slave culture and community. The historians' emphasis on re-sistance as the "primary shaper of cultural patterns" among slaves, for example, obscures the dynamics and diversity of slave folklife. Joyner offers his own model of cultural adaptation among Ameri-can slaves. He also invites students of slavery to study language, costume, food, architecture, technology, and material culture as clues to the mutability and meaning of slave folk culture. In some ways, Joyner's essay brings us back to Wood and Mullin. They had maintained that the enslaved Africans' material culture and work patterns reflected the values and social organization of the nascent slave "community," and they showed that material culture and work patterns, like all elements of culture, changed to respond to external forces such as the routinization of plantation labor or the end of fresh African slave importations. For Joyner, as for the other essayists, the slaves' culture was syncretic and dynamic, but for Joyner, more than the other essayists, its particular syncretism

Reprinted from Charles W. Joyner, "The Creolization of Slave Folklife: All Saints Parish, South Carolina, As A Test Case," *Historical Reflections/Reflexions Historiques*, VI (Winter, 1979), 435-453, without notes, by permission of the Managing Editor, and by the author.

and dynamism were rooted in place and time. Joyner thus cautions against making generalizations about the substance of slave culture and society for the whole South from limited, local resources. How do elements of culture, say material culture, change over time? Can, indeed must, historians extrapolate from local examples to make judgments about slavery generally? How might a local culture among slaves be carried to other parts of the South (what do the other essays suggest)? What is the role of the master in Joyner's model of acculturation? Finally, did the creolization process among American slaves point to cultural community or chaos?

ı

    Recent historians of slavery offer a refreshing, if still somewhat less than satisfactory vision of the nature and development of Afro-American culture. I believe we have finally reached the limits of the controversy framed a generation ago by the opposing conceptions of E. Franklin Frazier and Melville J. Herskovits. Frazier's assimilation model, emphasizing discontinuity with African origins and assuming acculturation to be the accommodation of Afro-Americans to Euro-American culture, was the dominant influence on a whole generation of sociologists as well as upon the mainstream of students of Negro history. In contrast, Herskovits emphasized the extent of Afro-American continuity with the African past, based upon his conception of the unity of West African culture. Herskovits has been influential upon a number of anthropologists and folklorists, and (at least indirectly) upon more recent historians of slavery who have posited African roots for Afro-American culture.

    The refutation of Frazier's assimilation model would seem by now to be as redundant an endeavour as yet another refutation of Sambo. Still the formulations of Herskovits and his disciples are not entirely satisfactory, either. Despite his recognition of such cultural transformations as syncretism, Herskovits' focus on the concept of "retention" is overly static and underestimates the dynamism of culture change. No group can transfer its culture intact from one environment to another. Both the natural and social context of the new environment will affect the nature and degree of cultural continuity, as will the circumstances of the migration. Moreover, Herskovits' concept of "Africanisms" is at once both overly abstract and overly concrete—abstract because it depends on

a notion of West African cultural homogeneity which is not supported by recent scholarship, and concrete because it fails to distinguish adequately between the concepts of "culture" and "society." Clifford Geertz's distinction between culture and society is
helpful in this regard. He defines culture as the mental rules gov-
erning behaviour, while society is the field of action in which behaviour takes place. For example, the concept of royalty is cultural, but the embodiment of that concept in monarchies and
courts is social. Societies are even less transferable than cultures
from one environment to another.[1] Because of their failure to distinguish adequately between culture and society, some historians
and social scientists have searched out vestigial concrete entities
and ignored basic perceptions and underlying principles. They have
looked for Africanisms in the wrong places. Cultural continuities
between Africa and Afro-Americans are strongest, as David Dalby
points out, "at the much deeper and more fundamental level of
interpersonal relationship and expressive behavior."

While recent historians of slavery, writing in the tradition of
Herskovits, certainly offer a more realistic view than that of their
predecessors in the Frazier-Stampp-Elkins school, their interpretation of the nature and development of Afro-American culture remains unsatisfactory. Their interpretation of its nature is dubious
because they stop short of conceptualizing the culture of the slaves
in holistic terms. Their interpretation of its development is dubious
because their concept of culture change is too monistic. In their
hands resistance becomes the prime shaper of cultural patterns
and complex processes of cultural change are reduced to a strat-
egy for survival. The challenge to historians is to transcend such
fragmentized and reductionistic interpretations of culture and of
culture change to come to a more accurate comprehension of the
nature and development of slave culture.[2]

A more accurate conception of the nature of slave culture is
the folklife model pioneered in this country by Don Yoder. Folklife, according to Yoder, designates "the total range of folk-culture
phenomena, material as well as oral and spiritual."

> Not only does the researcher study the verbal arts of folksong, folktale,
> riddle, etc.—which the folklorist has long ago made his province—but
> also agricultural and agrarian history, settlement patterns, dialectology
> or folk speech, folk architecture, folk cookery, folk costume, the folk
> year, arts and crafts. It is this exciting totality of the verbal, spiritual,
> and material aspects of a culture that we mean by the term "folklife."

A more accurate interpretation of the development of Afro-

American culture in slavery draws upon the concept of creolization. Creolization is a concept used in linguistic scholarship to explain the convergence of two or more languages into an essentially new native tongue. The earliest African slaves in any given New World area did not constitute a speech community, as the term is used by linguists. Their various African languages were often mutually unintelligible. The common language which they acquired was a pidginized form of English. Pidgins are developed as a means of communication among speakers of diverse languages. A pidgin is by definition a second language. It has no native speakers. When the pidgin was passed on to the next generation, it was their native tongue. While the parents remained bilingual, the principal language of the second generation was the pidgin, which, by definition, became a creole language once it acquired native speakers. The creole continued to develop in a situation of language contact, with reciprocal influence of English and African features upon both the creole and regional standard. The English contribution was principally lexical; the African contribution was principally grammatical.

The concept of creolization, applied to culture, focuses on the unconscious "grammatical" principles underlying human behaviour. It was such "grammatical" principles which survived the Middle Passage and mixed in the New World with elements of the masters' culture in the crucible of a new society to create a new creolized culture. It should be noted that the creolized culture was not static, either, but continued to develop in vigorous mutual interaction with that of the masters.

Not only have recent scholars of slavery been overly fragmented in their understanding of the nature of Afro-American culture and overly reductionist in their understanding of its development, they have been overly diffuse in time and space, painting on too broad a canvas for their evidence to be either conclusive or convincing. A bit of this from Mississippi, a little of that from Georgia, seasoned with a pinch of something else from Virginia, do not add up to an analysis of slavery in the South. "All events and experiences are local, somewhere," notes the poet William Stafford. How obvious, once baldly stated and explicitly perceived, and yet how little reflected in the writings of most historians. Too many historians attempt to describe and analyze wholes without having investigated concrete parts; too few construct wholes from empirically researched parts.

This study attempts to apply the concept of creolization to the study of slave folklife in a geographic area and in a time-frame limited enough for the varying kinds of sources to be mutually relevant and mutually revealing. Specifically, this is a study of slave folklife on the rice plantations of the Waccamaw Neck, All Saints Parish, Georgetown District, in the South Carolina lowcountry in the 1850s and 1860s. While I have made use of plantation records, visitors' accounts, census records, probate records, etc., the slaves' "grammar of culture" can never be comprehended using only sources emanating from their masters or their masters' guests. Despite the blatant assertion of George Fredrickson and Christopher Lasch that "slavery was an unrecorded experience, except from the master's point of view," there are numerous sources emanating from slaves which facilitate the study of their history "from the bottom up," including relatively untapped resources in oral tradition and material culture. This study is heavily based on oral traditions of three distinct types: 1) testimonies of ex-slaves who had experienced slavery on the Waccamaw Neck; 2) testimonies of the children and grandchildren of slaves on the Waccamaw Neck as to what information and attitudes were deemed important enough by the slaves to be passed on to their descendants regarding life in bondage; and 3) the testimony of folktales and legends, proverbs and songs from the Waccamaw Neck, which were not explicitly concerned with slavery but which, in conjunction with other evidence, yield crucial insights into the "grammar of culture."

Slaves on the Waccamaw Neck rice plantations lived and forged their culture within a distinctive economic, ecological, and demographic environment. They lived on larger plantations than slaves elsewhere. The smallest plantation in All Saints parish in 1860 had ninety slaves; the largest 1,121. The average number of slaves was 292. They lived in an environment virtually devoid of free blacks and of mulattoes, with a higher median age, a lower ratio of males to females, and smaller proportion of youth and aged than was true of the South as a whole. Perhaps most importantly, they constituted nearly ninety percent of the population throughout the mid-nineteenth century. In this regard the South Carolina lowcountry appears to be more nearly Caribbean in character than like other parts of the United States. The impact of the lopsided racial imbalance of culture change was momentous. It is true, as far as it goes, that the slaves were socialized into the ways their masters would have them behave, but it is also true that the heavy demographic dominance of blacks promoted the convergence of diverse African cultures. The slaves both renewed and transmuted African cultural patterns while adopting and adapting European ones, all the while sloughing off patterns from either tradition which were no longer meaningful. Nor were blacks the only participants in the creolization process on the Waccamaw Neck. Initiation of the whites into the ways of the blacks was as inevitable as the other way around.

Language is the one indispensable ingredient in all human thought. One who would understand the folklife of Waccamaw Neck slaves must first attempt to understand their creole language, Gullah, for it was through Gullah that the slaves gave shape to their culture, communicated with and entertained one another, proclaimed their sense of community, and created for themselves a symbolic identity. The development of Gullah demonstrates the paradigm of creolization, first in the pidginization stage in which a number of African languages converged to form a grammar into which a largely but not exclusively English lexicon was poured, and secondly in the creole stage in which the new pidgin language became the native tongue of succeeding generations of rice plantation slaves (and thus a creole). Since the creole developed in a situation of language contact, it had by 1860 moved in various ways in the direction of the regional standard speech. Initiation of white Carolinians into Gullah linguistic patterns was as inevitable as into other aspects of Afro-American culture, given the preponderance of the black population. By 1860 the South Carolina lowcountry was linguistically more Caribbean than American, featuring a full-blown creole language alongside a regional variety which departed from the national standard in part because of the strong Gullah influence upon it.

Work patterns illustrate a particularly interesting example of cultural creolization on the Waccamaw Neck. On one level there was strong continuity with African patterns. Rice was introduced into South Carolina from Africa, and the early technological expertise was supplied by Africans, not Europeans. By the mid-nineteenth century, however, the economic networks and management techniques of the rice planters, including the "task system," had been superimposed onto the basic system of rice culture. The highly individualistic task system, in which each person was assigned a separate task to be completed without regard to the work of others, contrasted with African traditions of communal labour. Nevertheless, a tradition of quasi-communal labour underlay the task system, with slaves hoeing side-by-side, hoeing in tempo to singing, helping slower slaves keep up, all of which reflect an African communal orientation toward work. In addition, some technological features, such as the widespread use of hoes as all-purpose implements and the continuing use of hand-coiled "fanner baskets" after African models, reflected the continuing influence of African "grammars" upon the work patterns of field workers.

The earliest slaves had brought with them from various parts of West Africa highly developed technologies in metalwork, woodwork, leatherwork, pottery, and weaving. The contribution of skilled slave craftsmen and mechanics to the economic development of the plantations has yet to be adequately credited. Not only were these skills retained and handed down to children and grandchildren, but slaves responded eagerly to incentives to acquire new skills. As a general rule, young slaves aiming for plantation "professions" were apprenticed to senior craftsmen or craftswomen to be taught and trained. In some cases slaves were sent to Charleston or even to England to be taught particular skills, such as cabinetry. The skilled workers, especially the carpenters and mechanics, enjoyed considerable status, deference, and independence in their work patterns on the plantations, reflected in the esteem in which such skilled workers were held by black and white alike.

Planters also regarded house servants to be of a higher status than that of field hands. Slaves on the Waccamaw Neck generally seemed to have shared a sense of status identification ranging from house servants at the top through drivers and artisans on down to field hands. A wide variety of work patterns are subsumed under the general label house servant: butlers, cooks, valets, maids, waiters and waitresses, laundresses, and children's nurses, among other occupations. House servants generally had lighter work than field hands on the rice plantations, but their closer contact with the master and mistress had both advantages and disadvantages. House servants were sometimes regarded as traitors by other slaves because of their more amiable relationships with the whites. In fact, however, house servants seem to have provided more runaways in All Saints Parish than field hands, perhaps because of their greater opportunities. The highly ambiguous situation of the house servants made it possible for them to occupy a special position between the "Street" and the "Big House" and to play an intermediary role in the creolization of each. They took African cultural patterns into the culinary, religious, and folkloristic patterns of the "Big House" and took European cultural patterns to the "Street." It was through the house servants that black Carolinians derived their European heritage, and white Carolinians their African heritage. The influence of the house servant was perhaps especially marked in the children's nurses—surrogate mothers, in many cases—whose role in the socialization process of white children was immense.

Among the rights successfully asserted by Waccamaw Neck slaves, "off times" and holidays became increasingly guaranteed. The temporal contexts set aside as "off times" were based on four overlapping cyclical concepts of time—the daily cycle, the weekly cycle, the annual cycle, and the life cycle. Within the task system, there was no uniform daily quitting time; slaves were not through for the day until they had completed individually-assigned "tasks." Many of them used part of their daily off-time to cultivate their own plots and raise livestock, both for their own consumption and to sell to the planters. Such purchases from slavery were contrary to South Carolina law, as the planters clearly understood; but they were part of the body of rights asserted successfully by the slaves even in the face of specific legislation to the contrary. Slaves who could accomplish two tasks in a single day received a full day off. Those who did so often used the time for fishing, clamming, and oystering. Saturday afternoons and Sundays were also used extensively for fishing and hunting. Sunday was a day of rest from the fields. Most slaves attended church services on Sundays, and many of them also held weekly mid-week prayer meetings and daily family devotions. Saturday nights were often given over to dances and social get-togethers, with entertainment by talented slave fiddlers, banjo players, and storytellers. Slaves who could obtain passes, or "tickets," could visit friends or relatives or go courting on other plantations. Some went visiting or courting without passes, braving the danger of being caught by patrols and beaten. The weekend visiting and partying both gave expression to African cultural patterns and promoted their continuing creolization. In the annual cycle, no holiday was more important than Christmas, when three days were set aside for celebration, feasting, gingerbread and sweets, extra rations, portions of rum or whiskey and tobacco, gifts, fireworks, and much singing and dancing. Lifecycle celebrations, such as weddings and funerals, were marked by special patterns of expressive behaviour which also reflected the slaves' creative adaptation of African customs and beliefs to New World conditions, under the influence of a Christian theology which the slaves subtly modified to accommodate persistent African cultural grammars. Partly through their use of off-times, then, Afro-Americans even within the House of Bondage carved out sufficient emotional space to further the development of their rich folk culture.

Attempts to discover the inner cultural grammars of the slaves will remain egregious speculations until careful examination is made of the stories told one another in the master's absence. My analysis of folktales on the Waccamaw Neck concentrates on human and animal trickster tales, their explicit and implicit themes, their structures, and their functions and uses in the slave community. Trickster tales are not unique to African and African-derived cultures; on the contrary, trickster tales occur universally. But they are not universally alike. Slave trickster-tales on the Waccamaw Neck exemplify tale-types and include motifs which are widely diffused throughout Europe and elsewhere. However, there are strong structural and thematic resemblances between African and Waccamaw Neck animal trickster-tales.

There are numerous relationships between the animal and human trickster-tales, but we must take care not to emphasize the similarities out of proportion. To miss the identification of Buddah Rabbit as a surrogate slave (on one level) is to miss the essence of the tales' central meaning to the slaves; however, other levels of meaning can be obscured by overreliance on the identification orthodoxy. Buddah Rabbit, Buddah Pa'tridge, and other animal tricksters do not serve exclusively as surrogate slaves, nor as role models to be followed in all cases. Such characters demonstrate both the advantages and the limitations of the trickster role. The trickster usually (but not always) accomplished his ends; but to do so he often has to become as cruel and vicious as his oppressors. He also seems to become as arrogant and as stupid as they; for when he is defeated, it is usually by the wiles of smaller and frailer (but trickier) creatures than himself. Thus the trickster served the slave community not merely as an example to emulate, but one to avoid as well.

The human trickster—usually the slave, John—is less ambiguous and complex than the animal trickster on the Waccamaw Neck, perhaps mainly because of his more clear-cut identification as one of the slave community. On the Waccamaw Neck (unlike John tales elsewhere, as Richard Dorson's large collection has shown), John does not lose any contest to the master. John does occasionally trick the weak as well as the powerful in the Waccamaw Neck tales (a realistic touch), but is never outwitted by weaker and shrewder characters. Such folktales as these were used as entertainment, but served both educational and psychological functions. They exhibited important lines of continuity with African tradition, as well as syncretic reinforcement from Euro-American culture, and the marked influence of the immediate social environment upon the creative process of creolization. They are eloquent testimony that at least some minds remained free even while their bodies were enslaved.

Material culture—the underlying "deep structure" which generates tangible objects—is an important and barely tapped historical source. Foodways, for example—the choice of particular foods or particular means of preparing foods—may have cultural and ideological significance beyond mere subsistence, may involve issues of crucial importance to a group's sense of identity. There are reciprocal relationships between food, culture, and society. Societies are shaped in part by the basic human need for food, but the activities and relationships of any social group shape their cultural concepts of hunger and appetite. The planters of All Saints Parish described their slaves as "bountifully fed," and most of the living ex-slaves interviewed for the Federal Writers Project slave narratives said their own masters were good providers. Some of them, however, indicated that not all Waccamaw Neck slaves were so fortunate as they. One ex-slave noted, "Doctor Magill people hab to steal for something to eat." My interviews with children and grandchildren of All Saints slaves indicated a rather greater degree of slave dissatisfaction with the plantation cuisine. Many a meal, I was told, consisted of nothing more than corn meal mush and molasses. Often the morning and evening meals were eaten at home in the slave houses, while the midday meal (and sometimes the morning meal) was eaten at a central eating shed or in the field. Cooking for the slaves in the public-pots was crude; and utensils for eating were as crude as implements for cooking, where they existed at all. The masters' allowances were supplemented with fruits and vegetables from the slaves' small garden plots. Hunting and fishing both supplemented the allowances and provided one of the slaves' few recreations. Weddings, Christmas and sometimes other holidays were occasions for elaborate feasts on some plantations. The use of alcohol by slaves was strictly limited to such occasions, but from time to time some slaves found both incentive and opportunity to imbibe anyway. The significance of food to the slaves is perhaps best revealed in two of their proverbs: "Hunger tame wild beast" but "a full belly makes strong arms and a willin' heart."

Costume is one of the basic symbols in any community, expressing not only its structure but its innermost values as well. Planters and visitors in All Saints Parish described the slaves as "bountifully clothed." Ex-slave testimonies and oral tradition reveal that the slaves were, for the most part, adequately clothed. Some clothing was purchased ready-made, but most planters ordered woolen cloth from England and had clothing made by full-time slave seamstresses on the large plantations. Cloth was also woven on the plantations by full-time slave weavers. While the slaves never had unrestricted choice in clothing, *how* clothing is worn is as culturally marked as *what* clothing is worn. Clothing behaviour marks age, sex, religious, marital, and status distinctions within folk communities. Among slaves the status distinction most clearly marked by clothing was that between house servants and other slaves. The white handkerchief, or bandanna, marking the high status of children's nurse, appears to be related to a West African practice expressing a high degree of personal pride. Patterns of clothing behaviour also marked distinctions among various social contexts in slave folklife, from everyday and occupational to erotic and ceremonial. The same rhythmic alternation between work and festivals that is evident in so many folk communities is symbolized in clothing. For Waccamaw Neck slaves that alternation distinguished between the workaday world of the weekdays and the festive air they gave to the weekends—a distinction between the time claimed by their masters and the time available for their own purposes. Slaves washed themselves and put on their best for Saturday night visiting or partying (or both) and for church on Sunday. Clothing behaviour is an important way of expressing group consciousness; during the week the slaves belonged to the master, but on Sundays they demonstrated their mutual respect and solidarity as members of a cultural community.

Henry Glassie and others have used folk architecture successfully as a means of penetrating artifactual "grammars" of people in past time. Unfortunately, most of the material remains of the old rice plantations have long since vanished. Julia Peterkin noted as early as 1933, "Many of the plantations have passed away so completely that no sign of them remains except in old graveyards whose sunken weeds and broken stones are overgrown and hidden by trees and rank weeds." Housing patterns reflected the masters' view of the slaves' social status. Behind the Big House stood the kitchen, and behind the kitchen were the cabins of the house servants. Behind them were the barns, stables, carriage houses and other plantation out-buildings. Further back was the "Street"— the homes of the field hands. The prevalence of single family dwellings would seem to have had an influence on the nature of family patterns and helped to promote a sense of community among the various residents of the "Street."

Thus various cultural influences converged within the slave community of All Saints Parish. The slaves' pidginized African cultural grammars directed their selective adoption and adaptation of elements of Euro-American culture to form a new creolized culture of their own. This study, by demonstrating the value of creolization theory and the holistic folklife concept to the comprehension of that process, points toward an approach to slave studies which I believe to be essential. The time has come to move away from the purely descriptive mode toward an analytical approach which poses issues germane to the understanding of culture and of its relation to society and to change. The time has come to move from sweeping surveys of broad areas and long time spans to close, careful studies which preserve the precise integrity of historical place and time. If the study of slavery is to move forward with the same intellectual excitement which has characterized its recent development, then broader (but inevitably shallower) comparative studies must be balanced by narrower (and, one hopes, richer and deeper) micro-studies. If these micro-studies are to be indeed richer and deeper, they must combine greater methodological and theoretical sophistication with closer attention to concrete realities. Clearly the concepts of creolization and of folklife have much to contribute to that development.

NOTES

1. Thus when John Blassingame charges historians with being simplistic for describing slave social structure as imposed from without he fails to distinguish between culture and society. He is certainly correct in emphasizing the importance of understanding the slaves' value system in terms of what was considered important by the slaves themselves, but value systems are cultural, not social. See his "Status and Social Structure in the Slave Community" in this volume.

2. For instance, Blassingame ignores the development of the creole language of the slaves, Genovese and Wood the slaves' songs and tales, Levine their material culture. Gutman focuses on a single cultural institution—the family.

Suggestions for Further Reading

The best way to understand the slaves' world is to consult the testimony of the slaves. Due to assiduous collecting by folklorists and historians, the body of slave testimony is surprisingly large and rich. Slave autobiographies from the nineteenth century are particularly abundant and useful. Charles H. Nichols, *Many Thousand Gone: The Ex-Slaves' Account of Their Bondage and Freedom* (Leiden, 1963), has a good list of the fugitive slave narratives. John Blassingame, *The Slave Community: Plantation Life in the Antebellum South* (New York, 1972), includes the fullest bibliography of nineteenth-century slave autobiographies and makes a strong case for their reliability. In the revised and enlarged edition of his *Slave Community* (1979), Blassingame extends his arguments on the utility of such sources. See also his important essay, "Using the Testimony of Ex-Slaves: Approaches and Problems," *Journal of Southern History*, 41 (1975), 473-492. Good collections of slave autobiographies include the following: John F. Bayliss, ed., *Black Slave Narratives* (New York, 1970); Arna Bontemps, ed., *Five Black Lives* (Middletown, Conn., 1971); Arna Bontemps, ed., *Great Slave Narratives* (Boston, 1969); Gilbert Osofsky, ed., *Puttin' on Ole Massa* (New York, 1969); Maxwell Whiteman, ed., *Afro-American History Series* (10 vols., Wilmington, Del., 1970); Robin Winks, ed., *Four Fugitive Slave Narratives* (Reading, Mass., 1969). No student should miss Frederick Douglass, *A Narrative of the Life of Frederick Douglass, an American Slave, Written by Himself* (Boston, 1845), which is the best slave narrative. Douglass expanded his account into *My Bondage and My Freedom* (New York, 1855).

In the 1920s and 1930s black scholars conducted interviews with ex-slaves and recorded their findings in several works: John B. Cade, "Out of the Mouths of Ex-Slaves," *Journal of Negro History*, 20 (1935), 294-337; Fisk University, *God Struck Me Dead: Religious Conversion Experiences and Autobiographies of Negro*

Ex-Slaves (Nashville, 1945); Fisk University, *The Unwritten History of Slavery: Autobiographical Accounts of Negro Ex-Slaves* (Nashville, 1945); and Orland Kay Armstrong, *Old Massa's People: The Old Slaves Tell Their Story* (Indianapolis, 1931), which is underused, but very useful. The fullest collection of interviews, autobiographies, and other personal accounts of slaves recorded before the 1930s is John W. Blassingame, ed., *Slave Testimony: Two Centuries of Letters, Speeches, Interviews, and Autobiographies* (Baton Rouge, 1977). Other important sources are letters written by literate slaves. Randall M. Miller, *"Dear Master" : Letters of a Slave Family* (Ithaca, N.Y., 1978), traces a slave family's life over two generations. Other good collections are: Robert S. Starobin, ed., *Blacks in Bondage: Letters of American Slaves* (New York, 1974); and Carter Woodson, ed., *The Mind of the Negro as Reflected in Letters Written during the Crisis, 1800-1860* (Washington, D.C., 1926). Many slave letters remain unpublished.

The most complete sampling of ex-slave testimony is the slave narrative collection conducted in the 1930s by the Federal Writers' Project of the W. P. A. George Rawick has compiled the narratives deposited in Washington in his 18 volume set, *The American Slave: A Composite Autobiography* (Westport, Conn., 1972). In 1977 he added twelve volumes of interviews which had been lost, suppressed, or unprocessed by the W. P. A. workers. In 1978 Rawick brought more interviews to light. Rawick's investigations led to the publication of numerous other W. P. A. ex-slave interviews which had not been deposited in Washington. Charles Perdue, ed., *Weevils in the Wheat* (Charlottesville, 1976), published Virginia narratives to supplement the accounts in *The Negro in Virginia* (New York, 1940). Ronald Killion and Charles Waller, eds., *Slavery Time When I Was Chillun down on Marster's Plantation* (Savannah, 1973), adds to the Georgia collection. On Georgia see also Tom Landess, ed., "Portraits of Georgia Slaves," *Georgia Review*, 21 (1967), 126-132, 268-273, 407-411, 521-525, and *ibid.*, 22 (1968), 125-127, 254-257. Ronnie C. Tyler and Lawrence R. Murphy, eds., *The Slave Narratives of Texas* (Austin, 1974), recovers Texas narratives. Louisiana narratives were not sent to Washington. Some were used in Lyle Saxon, comp., *Gumbo Ya-Ya: A Collection of Louisiana Folktales* (Boston, 1945). Margaret Dalrymple of Louisiana State University is collecting the narratives newly discovered in Louisiana archives. The best general selection from the W. P. A. narratives is Norman Yetman, ed., *Life Under the "Peculiar Institution": Selections from the Slave Narrative Collection* (New York, 1970).

A balanced account of bondage requires searching in records left by planters, travellers in the South, and other contemporary non-slave observers. Such documents help to define the structure of slavery as a labor and social system, and by recording the interaction of whites and blacks, they help to show the slaves' public posturing. The best collections of documents about slavery, both weighted toward the interior view of bondage, are Michael Mullin, ed., *American Negro Slavery: A Documentary History* (New York, 1976); and Willie Lee Rose, ed., *A Documentary History of Slavery* (New York, 1976). The commentary in both volumes is superb, and the selections are judicious and broad-ranging.

As the essays in this book demonstrate, written sources alone fail to capture the fullness and subtleties of slave culture. Black folklore and music especially reveal the values of the slaves. The most basic collection of spirituals remains William Francis Allen, Charles P. Ware, and Lucy McKim Garrison, *Slave Songs of the United States* (New York, 1867). Lydia Parrish, *Slave Songs of the Georgia Sea Islands* (New York, 1942), is useful. Two important collections of spirituals are James Weldon Johnson and J. Rosamond Johnson, eds., *The Book of American Negro Spirituals* (New York, 1925) and their *Second Book of Negro Spirituals* (New York, 1926), both reprinted in *The Books of American Negro Spirituals* (New York, 1956). Black folklore is most accessible in J. Mason Brewer, ed., *American Negro Folklore* (Chicago, 1968); Richard M. Dorson, *American Negro Folktales* (Greenwich, Conn., 1967); and for earlier recordings, A. M. F. Christiensen, ed., *Afro-American Folklore; Told Round Cabin Fires on the Sea Islands of South Carolina* (Boston, 1892). The various collections of ex-slave narratives, listed earlier, contain much slave folklore uncorrupted by time and editing of third parties.

The secondary literature on slavery, like the institution itself, seemingly has no natural limits. A complete bibliography of slavery in the United States is beyond the scope of this assignment. The books and articles mentioned below suggest the major works and trends in the literature on slavery, particularly on aspects of the social history of the institution. Students who want fuller bibliographical coverage should consult the appropriate sections in James M. McPherson, *et al, Blacks in America: Bibliographical Essays* (Garden City 1971), a rich and rewarding book; and Allen Weinstein, Frank Otto Gatell, and David Sarasohn, eds., *American Negro Slavery: A Modern Reader* (3rd ed., N.Y., 1979).

The modern debate over slavery began with Ulrich Bonnell Phillips' impressive, if deeply flawed, book, *American Negro Slav-*

ery: *A Survey of the Supply, Employment and Control of Negro Labor* (New York, 1918). Phillips' broad knowledge of southern agriculture and his command of the primary sources still make his contribution useful, but his assumptions about black racial inferiority and his conclusions about the benevolence of slavery, which he styled variously as a school and a "chapel of ease" for the enslaved, seriously weakened his arguments. In his *Life and Labor in the Old South* (Boston, 1929) Phillips modified some of his harsh judgments about black inferiority and the "benign" qualities of bondage. Phillips' classification of the subjects of slavery and his arguments about slavery's burdens for the masters continued to influence scholarship for twenty years and more. A number of black historians immediately took issue with Phillips' judgments, and scores of anthropologists, sociologists, and economists entered the lists to debate the effects of bondage on the enslaved and the profitability of slavery. For our purposes, the most important issue turned on the degree of African cultural survival among black slaves. Melville Herskovits made a strong case for significant African cultural survivals among New World blacks in his book, *The Myth of the Negro Past* (New York, 1941). Herskovits assembled much evidence to show that black folklore, music, religion, family structure, and social behavior owed much to their common African origins. Slavery had not stripped Afro-Americans of their African past. E. Franklin Frazier, while rejecting U. B. Phillips' assumptions about black inferiority and the educational benefits of slavery, conceded that the dominant Anglo-Saxon culture of the masters and the debilitating social effects of bondage, which disrupted slave family life and invaded black religion, overwhelmed the African slaves. The black slaves adopted pale imitations of white religion, family, and social values because their Old World culture(s) were ineffective or inappropriate in the New World setting. On Frazier's arguments see his books: *The Negro Family in the United States* (Chicago, 1939); *The Negro in the United States* (rev. ed., New York, 1957); and *The Negro Church in America* (New York, 1964). Thus framed, the debate on African cultural survivals raged thereafter. The issue underscored all assumptions about the social and cultural effects of bondage on the enslaved. The best place to follow the literature on the debate is in McPherson, *et al, Blacks in America*, pp. 32-39.

Phillips' influence continued, however, as many scholars eschewed discussions of the effects of slavery on the slaves and their culture and concentrated on plantation management, agricultural operations, the planter class, and the economics of slavery. The major reassessment of slavery by Kenneth Stampp, *The Peculiar Institution: Slavery in the Antebellum South* (New York, 1956), did not wholly escape this emphasis, but it did offer a point-by-point rebuttal of Phillips' major arguments. For Stampp, slavery was a factory. The institution was harsh and exploitive, and it turned a nice profit for the masters, who exacted a heavy human toll from the slaves. Stampp's book represented a major turning point in the historiography of slavery, for it effectively laid Phillips' arguments to rest. Thereby, it encouraged new avenues of discussion.

New questions about slavery arose quickly—none more important than the question of what slavery did to the slaves. Much of the literature on slavery since 1960 is a response to the work of Stanley Elkins, *Slavery: A Problem in American Institutional and Intellectual Life* (Chicago, 1959, 3rd. ed. 1976). Elkins stressed the comparative dimension of slave history by setting his discussion in the larger framework of New World slave societies, and, more importantly, he pushed forward the issue of the impact of the slave environment on slave personality. The question of slave personality excited the most controversy. Elkins argued that the severity of the slave regime, which was a total, closed psychological and cultural system imposed on the blacks, crippled the slaves' personality and robbed them of a distinctive culture. The repressive system, which Elkins likened to Nazi concentration camps, left no room for social or psychological maneuvering. They succumbed to the pervasive, massive power of the planters and became childlike, dependent creatures grovelling for the master's approval. The slave emerged from bondage as a Sambo.

Elkins' arguments ignited a furious debate about slave personality. Scholars criticized Elkins for misapplying the concentration camp analogy, for slavery was not a closed system. They charged that Elkins confused role *playing* with the internalization of roles. They pointed out that he neglected black sources in describing slave personality and culture. And they insisted that slaves were not set in any one mold, that slave behavior varied according to time, place, occupation, personality, and conditions of bondage. Much of the best literature on slave resistance as it relates to Elkins' thesis is available in Ann J. Lane, ed., *The Debate Over Slavery: Stanley Elkins and His Critics* (Urbana, Ill., 1971). Also important are: Kenneth Stampp, "Rebels and Sambos: The Search for the Negro's Personality in Slavery," *Journal of Southern History*, 37 (1971), 367-392; Mina Davis Caulfield, "Slavery and the Origins of Black Culture," in Peter I. Rose, ed., *Americans from Africa*

(2 vols., New York, 1970), I, 171-193; and Joseph Logsdon, "Diary of a Slave: Recollection and Prophecy," in William Shade and Roy C. Herrenkohl, eds., *Seven on Black: Reflections on the Negro Experience in America* (Philadelphia, 1969).

Elkin's arguments generated much interest in acculturation and slave responses to bondage. Indeed, almost every major work on slavery in the United States attempts to respond to Elkins' arguments, however indirectly. Much of the recent work on slave culture and slave personality has been enhanced by the rigorous application of social science methodologies and, more importantly, by probing analysis of slave narratives, folklore, and music. John W. Blassingame, *The Slave Community* (1972), mined slave autobiographies to demonstrate that slave personality ran the gamut from submissiveness to rebelliousness. Blassingame discovered a vigorous slave culture in the quarters, which offered the slaves alternative roles and values to counter the baneful influence of the masters. Blassingame described a healthy slave family and a powerful slave religion standing against the master's efforts to disrupt slave life. Blassingame's arguments did not go unchallenged, most particularly for his failure to appreciate the role of women and of occupation in determining the slave community's character, but scholars generally accepted his conclusion that a separate slave community grew in the quarters to insulate the slave from the master. The reactions to Blassingame's work are represented in Al-Tony Gilmore, ed., *Revisiting Blassingame's The Slave Community: The Scholars Respond* (Westport, Conn., 1978). Blassingame revised his work to meet the criticisms and to incorporate new material in the revised and enlarged edition of *The Slave Community* (1979). Blassingame's work was one of several studies appearing in the 1970s which treated slave acculturation and responses to servitude. Other useful works include: George Rawick, *From Sundown to Sunup: The Making of the Black Community* (Westport, Conn., 1972); James H. Dorman and Robert R. Jones, *The Afro-American Experience: A Cultural History Through Emancipation* (New York, 1974); Leslie H. Owens, *This Species of Property: Slave Life and Culture in the Old South* (New York, 1976); Nathan I. Huggins, *Black Odyssey: The Afro-American Ordeal in Slavery* (New York, 1977); and Paul D. Escott, *Slavery Remembered: A Record of Twentieth-Century Slave Narratives* (Chapel Hill, N.C., 1979).

The debate on slave culture and personality went parallel to questions about the profitability of slavery. In 1974 the issue of the slave economy attracted national attention with the publication of Robert W. Fogel and Stanley L. Engerman, *Time on the Cross: The Economics of American Negro Slavery* (Boston, 1974). The authors used computerized analysis to describe southern plantation slavery as profitable for both master and slave. Their conclusions about the physical treatment of slaves, particularly their insistence on work incentives and a high rate of material return for slaves supposedly imbued with a Protestant work ethic, surprised most students of slavery. Major rejoinders of *Time on the Cross* include: Herbert Gutman, *Slavery and the Numbers Game: A Critique of "Time on the Cross"* (Urbana, Ill., 1975); and Paul A. David, *et al, Reckoning with Slavery: Critical Essays in the Quantitative History of American Negro Slavery* (New York, 1976). Whatever their weakness in sampling, methodology, and argument, Fogel and Engerman did remind students that the culture of slavery was closely related to the economic functions of slavery.

If Phillips, Stampp, and Elkins dominated scholarship in their respective days, Eugene Genovese is likely to do so for ours. In numerous essays and several books published in the 1960s and 1970s Genovese sketched the contours of a major new interpretation of slavery and the slaves. For Genovese, it was impossible to understand the slaves without understanding the masters, and vice versa. Masters and slaves shaped each other's worlds even as they attempted to create their own separate worlds. Genovese brought together the strands of his thinking in his monumental book, *Roll, Jordan, Roll: The World the Slaves Made* (New York, 1974). He argued that a paternalistic ethos pervaded the plantations. This paternalism was used by the slaves to manipulate the masters and so to gain valuable social space to build their own religion and culture, but the slaves' "acceptance" of planter paternalism siphoned off any revolutionary currents among the slaves. Genovese offered many new insights about the slaves' sense of time, about the internal structure of the slave community, about the slave family, but particularly about slave religion. Religion was the most salient expression of an emerging Afro-American nation in slavery, but it was also a reflection of the limits of slave autonomy and power.

Lawrence Levine in *Black Culture and Black Consciousness: Afro-American Folk Thought from Slavery to Freedom* (New York, 1977) grasped the importance of religion and folk beliefs to understanding the particular culture blacks forged in America. He dismissed the argument over African cultural survivals as irrelevant and misleading by showing that the slaves created a distinctive

Afro-American culture based on their experiences and needs in this world, not on the tattered remnants of the Old World. As such, the culture was dynamic and responsive to the slaves' peculiar conditions.

The nature of the slaves' religion has occasioned a large literature. The best studies are: Albert Raboteau, *Slave Religion: The "Invisible Institution" in the Antebellum South* (New York, 1978); Donald Mathews, *Religion in the Old South* (Chicago, 1977); and Vincent Harding, "Religion and Resistance among Antebellum Negroes, 1800-1860," in August Meier and Elliott Rudwick, eds., *The Making of Black America* (2 vols., New York, 1969), I, 179-197. Other important studies include: Erskine Clarke, *Wrestlin' Jacob: A Portrait of Religion in the Old South* (Atlanta, 1979); Dena J. Epstein, *Sinful Tunes and Spirituals: Black Folk Music to the Civil War* (Urbana, Ill., 1977), a good addition to Levine's work; Vincent Harding, "The Uses of the Afro-American Past," in Donald R. Cutter, ed., *The Religious Situation* (Boston, 1969), 829-840; LeRoy Moore, Jr., "The Spiritual: Soul of Black Religion," *American Quarterly*, 23 (1971), 658-676; Randall M. Miller, "The Failed Mission: The Catholic Church and Black Catholics in the Old South," in Edward Magdol and Jon Wakelyn, eds., *The Southern Common People: Studies in Nineteenth-Century Social History* (Westport, Conn., 1980), 37-54; William C. Suttles, Jr., "African Religious Survivals as Factors in American Slave Revolts," *Journal of Negro History*, 56 (1971), 97-104.

The slave family has been the subject of intensive investigation in recent years. Most of the general studies cited above treat the slave family, but none go as far as Herbert Gutman's *The Black Family in Slavery and Freedom, 1750-1925* (New York, 1976) in arguing for the cultural autonomy of the slave family. Gutman roundly rejects Genovese's model of a paternalistic slave system and posits his own model of a slave family, and through it a slave culture, operating wholly independently of the master's knowledge or cultural influence. Other useful discussions of the slave family are: Robert Abzug, "The Black Family during Reconstruction," in Nathan Huggins, Martin Kilson, and Daniel Fox, eds., *Key Issues in the Afro-American Experience* (2 vols., New York, 1971), II, 26-41; C. Peter Ripley, "The Black Family in Transition: Louisiana, 1860-1865," *Journal of Southern History*, 41 (1975), 369-380; and for a very different, once standard, view, E. Franklin Frazier, "The Negro Slave Family," *Journal of Negro History*, 15 (1930), 198-259.

The nature of slave culture surfaced in a variety of ways. Good

discussions of how to use folklore, artifacts, music, and art to discover that culture and what that culture represented for particular
slaves are: Sterling Stuckey, "Through the Prism of Folklore: The
Black Ethos in Slavery," *Massachusetts Review,* 9 (1968), 417-
437; Robert F. Thompson, "African Influence on the Art of the
United States," in Armstead Robinson, ed., *Black Studies in the
University* (New Haven, Conn., 1969), 122-170; Lorenzo D.
Turner, "African Survivals in the New World with Special Emphasis
on the Arts," in John A. Davis, ed., *Africa from the Point of View
of American Negro Scholars* (Paris, 1958), 101-116; and Robert
Ascher and Charles H. Fairbanks, "Excavation of a Slave Cabin:
Georgia, USA," *Historical Archaeology,* 5 (1971), 3-17. Todd L.
Savitt, *Medicine and Slavery: The Diseases and Health Care of
Blacks in Antebellum Virginia* (Urbana, Ill., 1978), has some
interesting suggestions about health and culture.

The transmission of values reveals much about social structure
and culture. Thomas L. Webber, *Deep Like the Rivers: Education
in the Slave Quarter Community, 1831-1865* (New York, 1978),
discusses this much-neglected aspect of slave life. The retention of
values and culture after emancipation also can suggest much about
the substance of the slave community. Leon F. Litwack, *Been in
the Storm So Long: The Aftermath of Slavery* (New York, 1979),
is a major new synthesis. Roger L. Ransom and Richard Sutch, *One
Kind of Freedom: The Economic Consequences of Emancipation*
(Cambridge, England, 1977); and Joel Williamson, *After Slavery:
The Negro in South Carolina during Reconstruction, 1861-1877*
(Chapel Hill, 1965), will both profit the reader. No student should
miss Willie Lee Rose, *The Rehearsal for Reconstruction: The Port
Royal Experiment* (Indianapolis, 1964). Also important are: Peter
Kolchin, *First Freedom: The Responses of Alabama's Blacks to
Emancipation and Reconstruction* (Westport, Conn., 1972);
Edward Magdol, *A Right to the Land: Essays on the Freedmen's
Community* (Westport, Conn., 1977); and the essays by Willie Lee
Rose, Roger Ransom and Richard Sutch, and C. Vann Woodward
in David Sansing, ed., *What Was Freedom's Price?* (Jackson, Miss.,
1978). A good selection of documents is Dorothy Sterling, ed.,
*The Trouble They Seen: Black People Tell the Story of Recon-
struction* (Garden City, N.Y., 1976).

We know much about the end of slavery, but very little about
its beginnings in America. For the colonial period the best studies
of the impact of bondage on enslaved Africans are: Gerald Mullin,
*Flight and Rebellion: Slave Resistance in Eighteenth-Century
Virginia* (New York, 1972); and Peter H. Wood, *Black Majority:*

Negroes in South Carolina from 1670 Through the Stono Rebellion (New York, 1974). Also useful in this regard are Jeffrey Crow, *The Black Experience in Revolutionary North Carolina* (Raleigh, N.C., 1977); and Frank Klingberg, *The Negro in Colonial South Carolina: A Study in Americanization* (Washington, D.C., 1941). See also, Wesley Frank Craven, *White, Red, and Black: The Seventeenth-Century Virginian* (Charlottesville, 1971); Thad Tate, *The Negro in Eighteenth-Century Williamsburg* (Charlottesville, 1965); and the April, 1978, special issue of the *William and Mary Quarterly* on "Blacks in Early America." Two books on early racial attitudes and practices and the effects of race on American culture are Winthrop Jordan, *White Over Black: American Attitudes Toward the Negro, 1550-1812* (Chapel Hill, 1968); and Edmund S. Morgan, *American Slavery/American Freedom: The Ordeal of Colonial Virginia* (New York, 1975). See also, Carl Degler, "Slavery and the Genesis of American Race Prejudice," *Comparative Studies in Society and History,* 2 (1959), 49-66; Oscar and Mary Handlin, "Origins of the Southern Labor System," *William and Mary Quarterly,* 3rd series, 7 (1950), 199-222; Gary Nash, "Red, White, and Black: The Origins of Racism in Colonial America," in Gary B. Nash and Richard Weiss, eds., *The Great Fear: Race in the Mind of America* (New York, 1970), 1-26. For the broadest perspective on slavery and its New World origins, consult the magnificent books by David Brion Davis, *The Problem of Slavery in Western Culture* (Ithaca, N.Y., 1966) and *The Problem of Slavery in the Age of Revolution, 1770-1823* (Ithaca, N.Y., 1974).

Mobility and status within the slave community mirror slave culture and suggest the varieties of roles available to the slaves. There has been a recent surge of interest in so-called privileged bondsmen—artisans, drivers, houseservants. The most important studies are: William Van Deburg, *The Slave Drivers: Black Agricultural Labor Supervisors in the Antebellum South* (Westport, Conn., 1979), which addresses many other issues as well; Randall M. Miller, "The Man in the Middle: The Black Slave Driver," *American Heritage,* 30 (1979), 40-49; Robert Starobin, "Privileged Bondsmen and the Process of Accommodation: The Role of Houseservants and Drivers as Seen in Their Own Letters," *Journal of Social History,* 5 (1971), 46-70; C. W. Harper, "House Servants and Field Hands: Fragmentation in the Antebellum Slave Community," *North Carolina Historical Review,* 55 (1978), 42-59; Paul Cimbala, "Fortunate Bondsmen: Black 'Musicianers' and Their Role as an Antebellum Southern Plantation Slave Elite," *Southern Studies,* 18 (1979), 291-303; and Blassingame, *Slave*

Community (rev. ed., 1979); Genovese, *Roll, Jordan, Roll;* Miller, *"Dear Master"*; and Owens, *This Species of Property;* all cited earlier.

Not all slaves lived or worked on plantations. The most important studies of the "other slaves" are: Charles B. Dew, "Disciplining Slave Ironworkers in the Antebellum South," *American Historical Review,* 79 (1974), 393-418; Ronald L. Lewis, *Coal, Iron, and Slaves: Industrial Slavery in Maryland and Virginia, 1715-1865* (Westport, Conn., 1979); Robert S. Starobin, *Industrial Slavery in the Old South* (New York, 1970); and for a good collection of articles, James E. Newton and Ronald L. Lewis, eds., *The Other Slaves: Mechanics, Artisans, and Craftsmen* (Boston, 1978). On urban slavery, Richard Wade, *Slavery in the Cities: The South, 1820-1860* (New York, 1964), remains standard, but see also a recent challenge by Claudia Dale Goldin, *Urban Slavery in the American South, 1820-1860: A Quantitative History* (Chicago, 1976). One of the best books written about blacks in the South is Ira Berlin's, *Slaves Without Masters: The Free Negro in the Antebellum South* (New York, 1974). Berlin offers many useful observations on community building among blacks, free and slave, and pays particular attention to subregional variations in black social structure.

Slavery varied according to place. The most useful local and state studies of slavery include: J. Winston Coleman, *Slavery Times in Kentucky* (Chapel Hill, 1940); Robert McColley, *Slavery and Jeffersonian Virginia* (Urbana, Ill., 1964, rev. ed., 1973); Chase Mooney, *Slavery in Tennessee* (Bloomington, Ind., 1957); James B. Sellers, *Slavery in Alabama* (University, Ala., 1950); Julia Floyd Smith, *Slavery and Plantation Growth in Antebellum Florida, 1821-1860* (Gainesville, 1973); Charles S. Sydnor, *Slavery in Mississippi* (New York, 1933); Joe Gray Taylor, *Negro Slavery in Louisiana* (Baton Rouge, 1963); Orville Taylor, *Negro Slavery in Arkansas* (Durham, N.C., 1958); and the useful collection of articles in Elinor Miller and Eugene Genovese, eds., *Plantation, Town, and County: Essays on the Local History of American Slave Society* (Urbana, Ill., 1974). The chapters on slavery and social life in Guion G. Johnson, *Ante-Bellum North Carolina: A Social History* (Chapel Hill, 1937), will repay reading.

To appreciate the peculiarities of the southern experience and to grasp the fuller dimension of black adjustment to bondage generally, students should approach slavery from a comparative perspective. Good overviews of the enormous literature on slavery in New World societies are in the following collections: Laura

Foner and Eugene Genovese, eds., *Slavery in the New World: A Reader in Comparative History* (Englewood Cliffs, N.J., 1969); Michael Craton, ed., *Roots and Branches: Current Directions in Slave Studies* (Special Issue of *Historical Reflections*, Waterloo, Ontario, 1979); and David W. Cohen and Jack P. Greene, eds., *Neither Slave nor Free: The Freedmen of African Descent in the Slave Societies of the New World* (Baltimore, 1972). Students should consult Carl Degler, *Neither Black nor White: Slavery and Race Relations in Brazil and the United States* (New York, 1971); Harry Hoetink, *Slavery and Race Relations in the Americas* (New York, 1973); Herbert S. Klein, *Slavery in the Americas: A Comparative Study of Cuba and Virginia* (Chicago, 1967); Franklin W. Knight, *The Caribbean: The Genesis of a Fragmented Nationalism* (New York, 1978), the chapters on slavery and plantation society; C. Vann Woodward, *American Counterpoint: Slavery and Race in the North-South Dialogue* (Boston, 1971), especially the chapter on "Protestant Slavery in the Catholic World." David Brion Davis, "Slavery," in C. V. Woodward, ed., *The Comparative Approach to American History* (New York, 1968), remains the best introduction and the best summary of the principal issues on comparative slavery.